Winning Horseracing Handicapping

*Secrets of a Successful
Horseracing Handicapper*

Revised second edition published by
Lone Star Park at Grand Prairie
1000 Lone Star Parkway
Grand Prairie, Texas 75050

Cover photos by Skip Dickstein
Inside photos by Full Stride Productions.
Past performances copyright ©1999 Equibase.
Book design by Alan Gold, Fifth Leg Publishing.

ISBN 1-893793-02-8

Winning Horseracing Handicapping

Secrets of a Successful Horseracing Handicapper

Revised 2nd Edition

by

Chuck Badone

Fan Education Manager
Lone Star Park at Grand Prairie

Contents

Introduction

This book has been written for the benefit of every racing fan who has thrilled to the excitement of handicapping thoroughbreds, and to those who hope to begin handicapping. It is for the average fan. It is for you, and you, and you, and everyone who would like to win rather than lose.

I will impart my knowledge of horse racing, which has been gathered through forty years as a handicapper. I have taught full college courses in the art, conducted handicapping seminars at both Turf Paradise in Phoenix, Arizona and at Monmouth Park in New Jersey; and have been a member of the publicity staffs of both tracks, and am presently track handicapper at Lone Star Park at Grand Prairie.

This book is tuned to the common sense of every reader. The difference between good and bad handicapping is often knowledge. This book imparts the necessary knowledge of the principles of handicapping and the interpretation of these principles.

This book is *not* filled with statistics and charts. By the use of selected past performances or charts, I could prove any statistical fact, now matter how absurd. The few past performances shown in this book are used to illustrate a point so that you can recognize it when you see it.

After reading this, you need simply use your natural intelligence and common sense in applying these easy-to-understand principles. You need not be a mathematician or statistician—just have good judgement.

I have full confidence that upon finishing this book, you will be armed with the necessary knowledge to make you a winning horse player.

I thank God for the opportunity to have acquired this knowledge and for the ability to put it into words for your digestion. I appreciate the opportunity to have reached you.

CHAPTER 1

Prepare yourself for the races

Before becoming a serious student of handicapping, one must mentally be prepared to face the day-to-day battle of man over animal. If you plan to make racing a lifelong hobby, or a money-making venture, there are certain questions you must ask yourself and certain decisions must be made.

Basically, I feel a serious horse player must decide upon two major aspects of the sport. First, one must develop a philosophy regarding goals and aspirations; second, he or she must develop a method of *managing money*. The money-management method will generally coincide with the philosophy of the individual toward betting on horses.

I feel it is very hazardous to undertake handicapping horses as a hobby or a money-making venture without answering the above questions. It is especially important to *take stock of your financial position and gamble accordingly.*

One of the major pitfalls of gambling is betting money that you can't afford to lose—or, worse, don't have. I have always made it a point to take a similar amount of money to the track on a particular day. If I can afford to do without it, I'm not bad off. The old horse player's adage is, "I hope I break even; I need the money."

Although I don't wish to preach a negative attitude, one must not need his gambling money for food, clothing, and shelter—or any other bills he may have. Gambling with scared money brings on a great deal of undue pressure and can cloud one's thinking. Many bets you make are based upon decisions that are difficult enough to reach without the pressure of not being able to pay the rent if you lose. I in no way condone or recommend the so-called diseased gambler who gambles away the necessities while the family suffers.

Hopefully, everyone who embarks on a career of betting horses will know enough to back off when losing more than he or she can afford, and will have the sense to hold on to the money when winning. This all comes under the category of philosophy and money management, which I will elaborate on.

Philosophy

The word "philosophy" is not ordinarily used in connection with horse racing, but I find it very important. It is something that everyone who goes to the races has, but very few realize what it is. My feeling is that everyone who wishes to make horse racing a regular habit should have a well thought-out philosophy, and be able to recite it, and understand it.

One of the first things all racegoers should ask themselves is this: "What am I doing here, and what do I intend to accomplish?" Once this is answered, the fan can find the pattern of wagering that suits his personal philosophy.

One reason for going to the racetrack is very simply to make money. If you have these intentions, then you must gear your wagering to accomplish that thought. Another common objective of the race fan is pure recreational activity. One might say to himself, "I don't expect to win much, but I enjoy racing and the relaxation it affords." This, of course, brings another system of wagering into play.

You might have a combined philosophy that incorporates the two thoughts: you would *like* to make money, but would also like to have a good time. Some people play with only the thought of making money in mind, and still enjoy each day's racing. But most fans need the steady action of playing all or most of the races to really have fun, and this leads to a lessening of the profit potential.

The next chapter will deal with money management so I won't elaborate on how to apply your philosophy to your actual wagering habits at this time. But I will say that it is very important to understand your philosophy, and to know why you're at the races. When you have a clear understanding of this, you will be a happier horse player, seldom second-guessing yourself as to why you didn't skip this race or that, or why you didn't play this race or that. When you honestly know what your goal is, you can proceed to it. When you enter the gates to a race track say to yourself, "I'm here, and I know why."

Let players who love to play every race take heart. I, too, play every race, and have made a profit every year I can remember. I have thought about cutting down on the number of plays I make, but my philosophy dictates that I play them all.

Handicapping is my hobby, the only one I pursue with vigor, although there are other things I enjoy. I don't enjoy sitting out races, and although I realize I would be better off financially to do so, I have decided that my happiness is more important than the anticipated larger winnings. When I take the *fun* away from betting, I've lost a lot more than money. Money is important, but happiness is more important. I have asked myself, "What is it worth for me to be able to play every race?" And my answer is, "Quite a bit." Although I will never know exactly what it costs me in dollars, as long as I'm winning something and enjoying every race, this policy is worth it.

If you share my philosophy—and I know that many do—I can encourage you to do as you like; a profit can *still* be made when playing all the races. I am in no way advocating any single philosophy; however, players who play every race are often taking criticism from the disciplined player about how foolish it is to not sit patiently and pick your spots. I have taken plenty of criticism about my habits. I shrug it off because I know my goals and am satisfied with my results. More, no one can ask.

For those more patient people, let me say that I feel as excited about their way of doing it as I do about mine. If a person can pick his spots, enjoy his day, and make the kind of money he has envisioned, he, too, has a workable philosophy.

After gambling for a while, one usually realizes what the results must be to make *him* happy. If the desired results are not forthcoming, I suggest a change in tactics until the desired results are reached.

I have heard of people who profess to make a living at betting on horses. This, too, is a philosophy. I could never envision myself doing it, but I'm sure there are those who do. This is no longer under the heading of being a hobby, and may not even be fun. The gambler who wishes to make it his job will undoubtedly be under much more pressure as he must produce. Usually these people go to the track every day just as most people go to their jobs. He often makes no plays over an entire card. He must sit and wait for what he feels is a sure wager. My own feeling on this is that if the fun is taken out of it, then he is no better off than a person who goes to work every day. However, if he thoroughly enjoys this, can sit and wait for his spots, then his philosophy is as workable as anyone's.

Money management

Horse players and gamblers the world over have preached for years that money management is the key to successful gambling. Nothing could be more true. It can turn an excellent handicapper into a hopeless loser, and a relative novice into a money-maker. Managing your money is a matter of self-discipline. It is easier talked about than done, but there must come a time when you finally tell yourself, "I must develop a system of handling my money."

The big question is this—what system should be used? The answer is that the best system is any system that works for *you*. If you decide upon a method, and after a period of time you can logically see that it meets your demands, then stick with it. If it doesn't work, try something else. Only you know what your philosophy is and your method of reaching your goals must be your own. You can listen to horse player after horse player tell you of his way of managing his money, but rarely will their habits fulfill your needs.

As an example, if your philosophy was to go to the races once a week and all you hoped for was to break even, you might decide to play a $6.00-combine on a horse in each race. If, after a month you saw that you were indeed breaking even, and you were satisfied with the results, you would have found your money management system. If you decided on the other hand to spend every other day at the track with the sole intention of making money, you might decide to bet only certain races each day, and wager $50 to win on each selection. If you later found that you were winning as planned, you too have found a system.

There are many ways to skin a cat. You could conceivably come up with the most unorthodox method of wagering ever thought of, but it may be within your philosophy and meet your goals. If this is the case, then your money-management system is a good one.

This may take experimenting and thought. You may well want to listen to others, read books and gather any information you can pertaining to probabilities and statistics. *When you begin forming your method, remember that it must coincide with your philosophy.* It can be changed as you see certain adjustments must be made, or scrapped altogether if it isn't working, but any well thought-out system is better than none. If you have the self-discipline to stick to it, it will pay off in the long run. If you wish to be successful and meet your goals, you must develop self-discipline—or your road will be a rough one.

This may seem to be a contradiction. First I discuss lacking the discipline to play only selected races, then talk about how important self-discipline is in your wagering. Actually, *money is still the prime target.* You may resign yourself to the fact that you will win between $100 and $500 per year and no more, but you shouldn't settle for *losing* that much a year. Some people, just to bet, do lose each year, and feel it is well worthwhile, but the purpose of this book is to *turn the losses into winnings.*

I will now discuss some of the do's and don'ts of money management. One of the first rules you should follow is never to bring more money to the track than you intend to wager.

I have heard many a husband leave the house with the wife asking, "How much are you bringing?" "Just $150" is the reply. "But you usually only bring $100," retorts the wife. "I won't bet it all," says the husband. "I just want it with me." This, of course, is faulty thinking, because I've never seen a horse player have money in his pocket after losing his quota and not use the rest to try to get it back.

I suggest bringing about the same amount of money to the track with you each day. It should be something you can afford and enough to feel comfortable with. You don't want to bring too little or you will be pressing and not able to play the way you wish to. One of the big mistakes horse players make is to win $500 one day, then bring back $600 the next. If your habit is to take $100 with you each time you go, no matter how much you won the day before, bring back only what you usually take the next time.

The reason for this is obvious. Racing is a game of *percentages.* You can't expect to win all the time. After a big winning day, it is not likely that the next day will be as lucky. To go back and lose all you have won on your good day is foolish. If you take $100 per day, and win $500 on a given day, you should say to yourself, "After the next five trips, if worse comes to worse, I will still be even." If you should have a few bad days in between, and, say, lose $300, you are still $200 ahead. Then if your luck changes on the fourth day and you win another $200, you will be ahead $400 and in good shape.

I have said to myself on many occasions that if I had brought $1,000 to the track I would have lost it all. Some days you can't cash a ticket; nothing you do is right. Hopefully, on those days you just lose your quota and not what it had taken you weeks to win.

I once knew a man who had an unbelievable day on his first trip to the races. He brought with him only $40. He bet $10 on the first race and won. His bankroll jumped to $80. He then bet back $60 in the next race. This went on race after race. No matter how much he had, he would bet most of it back on the next race. As luck would have it, he hit the first seven races and went home. He won nearly $5,000 for his short stay at the track. The man asked the familiar question, "How long has this been going on?" The next time he went to the track, his tactics were the same, but the luck not as good. As expected, he lost what he had taken to the track in short order. I knew this man for many years and his pattern never changed. He still dreamed of the day he won every race, but it never happened again. He invariably went broke somewhere during the card. He may have had $500 in the fourth race, but by the seventh he would be asking if someone would like to split a dollar bet on a 30-1 shot.

People like my friend seem to have one basic philosophy: They bet until they lose. The chronic gambler who loses everything he owns is of this nature. No matter how much he won the day before, he will bet it all back the next day. Even if he gets on a hot streak, he will increase the size of his wagers until he finally loses it all. Don't be an I'm-going-to-bet-until-I-lose gambler.

Take approximately the same amount of money with you each time. When you've won, don't take more than you usually take the next day. Also, bet about the same amount on each race. If you are a $2.00 bettor, don't decide to be a $50 bettor after you have won on three races in a row. By that time, the percentages are against you, and even if you chose the right horse, he may lose.

One day you'll have the dream day when you start with $2.00 and end up betting $50, and you will win more than you thought possible. Unfortunately, victory plants the seed of defeat, and you will probably spend the rest of your horse-playing life trying to recapture that dream. In the meantime you have lost any chance to ever be a steady lifetime winner at the races.

It is a good idea to plan out your betting strategy beforehand. Decide what horses you will play and how much you plan to play on them *before* you get to the track. Just vary a few dollars, if at all, from the original plan.

You may want to play a few dollars more on a horse going off at larger odds than you expected, or shorter odds, but make it an amount within reason.

If I'm a $5.00 player and I'm ahead $80 after the seventh race, I should be able to feel that I will win at least $70 for the day no matter what happens in the last two races. *This is what is meant by money management.*

Have a pattern to follow.

Know what you can afford and what your comfortable betting limit is.

If you feel as if you're going to have a heart attack after every race, you're probably betting more than you can afford. Your money management system should make you feel that no matter how many bad days you've had, you will win it all back *if* you stick to your system of wagering.

If you're behind, don't panic and start playing 50-1 shots to get it all back at once. Stick to your pattern and hope to get at least some of it back; tomorrow is another day. Don't throw good money after bad. You can probably count on one hand the days you were hopelessly behind and then bailed out in the last race. It seems that when you are far behind, no matter how much you bet in the final two races, you lose. Instead of losing your usual $100, you borrowed $30 more to try to get even and lost that also.

When you have had a bad day, lick your wounds and come back another time. Remember, with quinella, exacta and all the other gimmick wagering going on, you're just one race away from being ahead.

In talking about gimmick wagering, the question becomes whether it is sound to play them. My feeling is that gimmicks are the savior of the $2.00 player. Never has a small bettor been able to make the money on one race that the big bettors have always been able to make. A $2.00 player can hit an exacta for $1,000 and have enough playing money for half the year *if* he continues to be a $2.00 bettor. Before the advent of gimmick wagering, I struggled year in and year out to break even. Trying to pick enough winners on a card to show a profit is not easy. When quinellas, exactas and trifectas came in, I could hit one race a day and make a lot of money.

This is based upon the theory that horse players would like to make large sums of money. If I were able to sit out seven races a day, then bet $50 to win on the other two races, I would have a chance to win a lot of money and wouldn't need the lure of exotic wagering. A player who bets $100 to win in a race can win thousands at one time. This player doesn't need the high risk of picking two or three horses in a race. But for the horse player who bets smaller sums, it is a great feeling to believe that you have a chance to win the big money without putting the big money out.

Quinella wagering is the easiest of the gimmick wagers to hit. In quinella wagering, you must select the first two finishers, but you need not pick the exact order of finish. The payoff is proportionately less, as one might expect, but a quinella often can pay large sums for very little investment. Here, you pick the first two finishers in either order. If you spend $6.00, you can box three horses. If two finish first and second in the race, you win.

Exacta wagering is the same as quinella—picking the first two finishers—but they *must* be in exact order. It costs $12.00 to box three horses, but the payoff is usually larger. Trifectas are also a craze. You need to choose the first three finishers in exact order. It is a very risky wager, but it has huge payoffs.

Then there is the old standard, the daily double—picking the winner of the first two races (or whatever races have been designated as the daily double races). I believe this to be the most difficult wager because you have to be right in two consecutive races and it is not easy. In quinellas, exactas, or trifectas, you need to have successfully handicapped just one race and you win. I find it easier to pick a winner and *then* try to find the second place horse than it is to pick two winners in a row.

One must learn to use discretion when he or she plays the gimmicks. Don't ignore your 20-1 shot to win while playing him in exactas only. Often the player will be overheard bemoaning his fate as he loved a 20-1 shot who won, used him on top in three exactas, but could not pick the second horse. When playing these races, you have to use a combination of the types of wagering available to you. Some races call for playing the gimmick, some call for playing the horse you like to win, or across the board. Many times, especially in quinella wagering, you play a 6-1 shot. It costs $10 to play the race, and you hit the quinella for $12.40 and the horse you liked won and paid $14.80 for $2.00.

In using the exotic wagers, you must learn to apply common sense as to what is your best wager for a particular race. It certainly makes things more complicated than the old win, place, and show. But it is also more exciting.

CHAPTER 2

Touts and tips

Every fan must decide how much stock to put into the various selectors on the grounds, or the tips one hears during the course of a racing card.

Let me say first that any serious handicapper worth his salt will pay little or no attention to the people who make selections on cards, in the newspapers, or in any other way. If one learns to handicap, and is reasonably confident in his ability, he should expect to make it on his own merits. If you win, you can thank your ability to handicap. If you lose, go back to the drawing board for another try on another day. If you are doing badly over a period of time, you probably need to improve your skills and knowledge of the game. Anyone who intends to make handicapping a serious hobby should learn to sink or swim on his own.

It is upsetting to lose a bet because you listened to someone else rather than rely on your own handicapping ability. I am sure the world's best handicappers have at one time or another let someone else's opinion influence their wagers—and then regretted it. It is one thing to lose because of a bad selection, but when you make the correct selection and go off of it for someone else's, it's probably the most exasperating experience in racing.

There are two types of information rampant around every racetrack. Many people make selections in print; they range from those who sell cards at the entrance of the track to the handicappers who make selections in *Daily Racing Form* and the local newspapers. The casual racegoer who has not mastered the art of handicapping to any extent may be aided by the handicappers. The information given by people who spend every day at the track is obviously better than using the hat-pin system. Novices or those who can't handicap and never intend to learn won't be hurt by the printed selectors.

In deciding which to use, be cautious when using *Daily Racing Form* selections in the selectors' box. Most selections are made by a handicapper not located at the track, so they don't offer any great insights. Closer looks are more meticulously done and more valuable. The trackman is on site, but often makes selections off the overnight.

Only those people who are very conscientious will take the time to look up old charts of previous races to aid them in making accurate selections. Many, I am sure—since they have nothing at stake—haphazardly and without much thought arrive at selections. There is really no way of telling which selectors are doing their homework. This makes use of their selections precarious.

Some writers who print their choices in the daily newspapers are conscientious racetrack fans; these can give you as good a set of selections as anyone. However, many local papers covering the sport assign men who care nothing about racing and do it only because it is an assignment. They know little about handicapping and spend a minimum amount of time in preparing their choices. To follow these selectors would be no better than using the hat-pin system.

The men who sell the "tip sheets" or cards outside a track entrance, or just inside the gate, are usually more reliable because they make their living at it. These people are there every day, which is an advantage in itself; they are fairly competitive with each other; and consequently each takes time and precautions in preparing his or her selections. Some may just be poor handicappers and their picks not worth the paper they are printed on. Others may be astute and come up with a decent percentage of winners. The only way to tell them apart is to keep records on how each does when you buy their cards. Don't go back to the poor ones.

To reiterate, the selectors are fine for those who need help. The student of the game should ignore them altogether and make it on his own.

Tips

Tips come in many ways, shapes, and forms. Most of them are said to emanate from the backstretch, direct from trainers, owners, or jockeys. Some are started by a fan who remarks to a friend, is overheard, and the whispers spread throughout the stands I can only say that nothing holds less water than information from a trainer, owner, or jockey—and especially from a fan.

I pay the smallest attention to a tip from the owner. An owner is very much like a father who has a son in the ball game—the son can do no wrong, is rarely at fault, and will always do better next time. Horse owners are, in general, very proud of their stock. Seldom does one believe that his horse has no chance to win, except in rare cases where the horse has been away from racing for a long time. Even then the owner has visions of a miracle happening.

To ask an owner how his horse will do in a certain race is like asking a father if his son is the best pitcher on his team. People who own horses are usually oblivious to the other horses in the race. Their partiality makes it difficult to see the merits of the other entries, and they usually wager on their own horses regardless of the competition.

I don't blame all those owners. It is natural to feel pride and I'd probably be the same way if I owned horses. As I don't, I never listen to an owner who tells me about the chances of his horse in a particular race.

Trainers are also very unreliable, although they are a little more realistic than the owners. Trainers are not handicappers. Rarely do you find a trainer who can handicap expertly as well. These people are much too busy getting their stock ready to run to be able to handicap races, in addition. A trainer is concerned with running the horse where he belongs and keeping him fit. Most trainers do not know from which horse the sternest opposition will come in a race They hope their horse runs his best race. That's what they work for and what they know.

I have received many bits of information from trainers in the past due to my position in the publicity departments of Monmouth Park and Turf Paradise. The number of times a trainer has touted me correctly could be counted on one hand. In fact, I knew one man who inadvertently gave me the opposite information on ten separate occasions. Five times he thought he would win and his horse performed poorly, and five times he didn't think he had much chance and his horse ran well. I don't believe that he was deliberately throwing me off because he was a good friend. Even if he was, it took no genius to see the pattern.

A friend of mind one day talked to the trainer of a particular horse and related the exchange to me.

"I asked the trainer why his horse ran so poorly last time after winning two straight before that," said my friend. "The trainer only answered by shaking his head, leading me to believe that he really didn't try to win. 'What is he going to do today?' asked my friend. The trainer slowly and knowingly nodded his head. The man never spoke a word, but his head shaking was as loud as if he'd screamed it over the loudspeaker."

I told my friend to be careful. The horse was nine-years-old, had won twice then was laid up for six weeks. His return was very dull and the horse had a history of being unsound. My friend could only remember that positive head shaking and ran up to make his biggest wager of the meeting. The horse finished dead last.

Jockeys are also very unreliable tipsters. Although they spend more time handicapping than a trainer, they only look for how the race shapes up so they can make a race plan. Jockeys are not allowed to gamble at the windows as are customers, and by law they are allowed only to have a wager on the horse they ride through the trainer or owner, and cannot initiate the wager. This discourages the majority of jockeys from trying to wager on a steady basis. It consequently cramps their handicapping skills.

Most jockeys 1 have known rarely will tell you they are definitely going to win. Most are usually uncertain and will say they have a good chance, they won't say much else. At some race tracks, scandals have arisen because of jockeys who bet and tried to fix races. I don't think that aspect of racing need be elaborated on because, for the most part, racing is very much on the up and up. Jockeys try to win with their mounts, have enough at stake in each race with the winners share of the purse, and have no more idea as to the winner as the average fan.

One other type of tip that you may encounter at a racetrack is the fan who has heard something from someone else. That should be taken for what it is worth--nothing. A man came to me recently to tell of a sure winner in an upcoming race. I asked him where he got his information and he told me it came from the man who ran the popcorn stand. My answer was that if the popcorn man knows it, and now you know it, then the entire racetrack must know it and the horse will be 2-5. A genuine piece of information will rarely get to the popcorn salesman or the average fan. If a trainer knows something, he usually keeps it to himself and his close friends.

One evening at Scarborough Downs in Maine I stood by the paddock railing inspecting the horses for the next race. I had had a bad night and was down to my last ten dollars. A man standing next to me glanced a few times then decided to impart to me some important information. "My friend," he said "you look like a nice guy. I'm going to tell you something, but don't breathe a word of it to anyone else. I drove all the way from Albany, New

York—300 miles—to play the two horse in this race. I know the trainer and the owner and, believe me, this horse is ready to win."

I looked back in my form and saw that I had already eliminated him from my wagering plans. He was an older horse that had run well once, but had been away for over a year. I looked at him in the paddock and he was bandaged heavily. He looked terrible. Why would this guy drive all the way from Albany to play him? I went out to look at the odds as the horses came on the track. He was bet down to 2-1, rather low for a broken-down animal. Ten dollars on him would get me back $30, and enough to play the rest of the night and recoup my losses. I forsook my original selection and placed the last precious ten dollars on number two. Then I tearfully watched him run last as my original selection won going away.

In summing up this chapter on touts and tips, I would like to mention the occasional time when backstretch information is valid. When you hear from a trainer that a particular horse will have an equipment change that is expected to improve him, it may be worth noticing. Also, a trainer or owner may reveal that the horse had been sick and has recently recovered and will run a much-improved race. This type of information can be important and may give you an edge over those who are relying on *Daily Racing Form*. And at times, a trainer will find something that makes a horse improve, and it can be backed by some better recent workouts. However, for the most part, handicapping—using good, sound principles that I'm going to tell you about—is the key to winning at the races and not inside information.

I might also mention at this time that equipment changes that are in the program, or announced over the loudspeaker, should always be taken as a positive sign. It may or may not help the horse, but the trainer is doing it to improve the horse's chances. As a handicapper, you must feel that a change made by a trainer is for the horse's improvement. It may hurt him, or it may help him, you will not know until he tries it. The trainer makes the change because he thinks it will help, or he is just experimenting. Either way, think of it positively.

CHAPTER 3

Physical condtion vs. conditions of the race

In trying to deduce the winner of a horse race, there are two basic questions to be answered, and every available piece of statistical data, or any other bits of information that can be gathered, all go into answering those two questions.

First, you must determine which horse is physically capable of winning the race. By physically capable I mean, which animal has his muscles toned and the wind capacity at a maximum?

The second answer to seek is: Who is capable of winning because of superior ability, and the conditions of the race? In other words, under normal conditions, who can beat whom in competition?

Physical condition

In looking at the aspect of physical condition, it is obvious that an animal, no matter how much ability he has, will not be able to win if he is in poor shape. It would only seem natural that a professional football team with only three days of practice would probably be beaten by a college team which had been finely honed after weeks of training.

There are two basic ways to determine physical condition through the data provided in *Daily Racing Form.* One is to look at how recently were the previous races. The other is through monitoring workouts.

How recent were the previous races? This is listed by giving the date and year of the last race. In determining fitness, the handicapper must check each date carefully to be sure that these are in the current year. At times, a horse will have run his last race in the same month—but of last year. A horse away from the races for a year is probably not in top condition.

You must also look for large gaps in the previous races. For example, a horse may have raced as recently as last week; but previous to that, have run months ago. You would then have to calculate whether the one race has put him into the necessary condition to be a factor. As a general rule, if a horse has had three races after a lengthy layoff, he should physically, at least, be capable of running his best.

The only other way, without talking to the trainer himself, to determine fitness is through workouts. These are printed at the bottom of his past performances. Just as in the case of an athlete, a horse can reach top physical condition by training. If a horse has been away for a long time, you must examine his workouts and decide whether or not he can exert a top effort. Analyzing workouts will be discussed in a later chapter.

It must be noted, however, that as in the case of human athletes, *competition makes a horse more fit than mere training.*

A horse that has not raced in a month, and shows no published workouts, is in questionable condition. So is a horse with a year layoff and many workouts. You can never be certain, except perhaps with the top class horses, whether a horse is in peak competitive condition through workouts alone.

Unfortunately, not all trainers train horses the same way. Some will give their horses long, slow gallops in lieu of clocked workouts between races. Even though the horse has not been out in a month, the trainer has kept him in running shape without published works. Unless you know the trainer and his style of training, you have a missing piece to the puzzle. This is an unknown factor that causes you to guess as to his true condition: it's a precarious situation to say the least. A serious horse player rarely guesses and seldom backs a horse under these conditions.

A successful handicapper must ascertain whether the horse is physically capable of winning or not. If the answer is obvious, such as a number of recent races, there is no problem. When it is not obvious, due to a lack of recent racing, or not enough training, this becomes a guessing game.

A horse is many times a real borderline case and he may or may not be fit. There are times you just don't know. A horse with a month's layoff may have been rested because of physical problems such as leg soreness and was unable to go to the track for workouts. The trainer enters him in a race knowing he will probably need the race for conditioning purposes. On the other hand, he may have been rested and galloped frequently—be in fine condition and benefited from the rest. If you wager on every race, you may take a chance on horse like this should the price be right (never do so on a favorite). He may win or finish dead last. Those who only spot their plays would never wager on this questionable horse.

Winning capability

Whether a horse is capable of winning is a much more complex problem for the handicapper. *It is actually the meat of his study.*

Being capable means being good enough, having the ability. Some horses in a race, in the peak of condition, with the best of racing luck, cannot run fast enough to win. Others could conceivably win if, in their best condition, enough good luck enters in. Then there are those which, when fit, are superior to the other horses and *will* win barring unforeseen circumstances.

The competition tells the story

In the forty years I have spent handicapping horses, I always wondered why some variables seem very important, but just when you latch on to a few winners, the variable that led you on to those winners leads you to twice as many losers. No one major thing seemed to make a difference, until one day I became enlightened after spending an evening at Scarborough Downs near Portland, Maine.

I had passed twelve consecutive summers in beautiful Maine, and each summer I was able to show a large profit on my wagering. I could not understand this because I couldn't do it for any length of time at any other track. While driving home one night after my tenth straight winning evening, the answer hit me. I knew why I could win at Scarborough with regularity. The reason was that I was there every night and had made, without realizing it, a mental categorizing of the ability of the horses on the grounds. In other words, I knew which were classier than others. Because Scarborough ran nine $1,500 claiming races each night, the average fan who vacationed in the area but only attended the races a few nights, had no way of telling the class horses in each race.

One might readily ask, if all races were $1,500 claiming races, what difference is there? The answer is obvious. There was a difference. All one thousand horses on the grounds could not be of the same quality. The only way to tell was to be there every night, know which horses each was up against when they ran, understand the conditions under which they ran, and to be able to quickly spot the difference.

It suddenly became quite clear to me. *It didn't make any difference what their time was in the last race, or the weight they carried, or the fractional time, or where they finished, or how far back they were—but which horses did they race against?* From this premise, I began thinking about other aspects of sports. This theory becomes obvious when you use human beings instead of horses.

Let me give some examples. First, take myself. I am older and not in good condition, although I was a former athlete and coach. If I were asked to race the jockey colony at a track over a distance of 200 yards, I would be beaten badly. A week later, I am asked to race the same distance against the office secretarial staff, forty years and older. If my last race was charted on paper, I certainly would look like a long shot, but I would probably win the race.

This is a gross exaggeration, but not that far out of line. It illustrates the point. It didn't make any difference where I finished or what my time was, but *whom I ran against.*

My time may have been much slower than in the following race simply because I was so hopelessly beaten that I didn't even try after the first part of the race. Although there is a great discrepancy between the jockey colony and the secretaries, it can be narrowed down to where I may have little chance against the jockeys, but a decent chance with a maintenance crew. When you continue to narrow it down, you may find that I can never defeat a certain group, but can always be close enough to win against another group.

What difference does this make? Take this example. The Oakland A's may finish in the cellar in the American Baseball League, but can whip their Pacific Coast farm affiliate eight out of ten times—even if their affiliate has won the Pacific Coast pennant. The records may have read A's 62-100, farm team 100-62, but who cares? All I want to know is: *Whom did they do it against?* A varsity will defeat the J.V. team almost every time regardless of their respective records.

If a boxer came to you and said that he had won twenty consecutive fights and that he wanted your prediction on his next engagement, you wouldn't ask him how many knockouts he scored, or where the fights took place. You would ask him: "Whom did you beat, and whom are you fighting next?"

If a baseball coach came to you and said that his team had won twenty straight and asked for a prediction on his next game, you wouldn't ask him for his statistical sheet. It wouldn't make any difference how many home runs the team had hit, or their batting averages, or their Earned Run Averages. The fist question would by, "Whom did you beat, and whom are you playing next?" *If* the level of competition was exactly the same, *then* I would want to see the statistical sheet to try to separate the teams.

In thoroughbred horse racing, many of the races are filled with horses who have competed against primarily the same type of opposition. But other races have horses entered which have raced against better competition, and some have faced far better than they are now facing on this given day. *When this is the case, and the horse is presently in good physical condition, he will win a large percentage of the time—and very often not be the favorite.*

As I get into the other variables, these will always relate to the one basic premise that the horse that has faced the best competition will, in a great many cases, be the horse to beat—regardless of any other factor except fitness. Finding the class of the race is not always as easy as it seems. In many cases it takes time and a knowledge of racing to understand which horse is actually the class of the race.

Let's take some time now to see the *ways* that class can be distinguished.

Claiming price

Probably the easiest way to tell which horses have met the better competition is by their claiming prices. If you handicap at track that runs claiming races from $5,000 to $35,000, most of the races will carry a tag that is easily discernible. Obviously, a $6,500 race has, for the most part, better horses in it than a $5,000 race.

There is usually enough of a difference between a race at the bottom of the claiming ladder, and the next notch up. Let's say a track has a bottom claiming price of $5,000; the next step up is $6,500. There is a greater difference here than meets the eye. The $5,000 race has the poorest claimers on the grounds in it. The best you can expect is a horse or two dropping down from $6,500, or possibly from $8,000.

Rarely do you get a fit horse dropping from $6,500 to $5,000. This means that the $6,500 race has mostly solid $6,500 horses in it, and some dropping from as much as $8,500. This makes it a much tougher race. When the $6,500 horse drops to $5,000 after a fourth-place finish, he may have lost to two $8,500 horses and a $6,500 animal. It certainly makes his chances look good against the bottom of the barrel.

The claiming price can fool you, however. One must recognize that some races for $6,500 are not better than a $5,000 race. For example, a $6,500 race for 3-year-olds may not be as good as a $5,000 wide-open race. A higher claiming race for fillies and mares or for horses bred in that state is usually no better than the claiming price just under it.

Any race that restricts the entrants is usually no better than the class just below it. (You may notice that I often use the words "usually" and "mostly" because in horse racing nothing is true all of the time). There are so many $3,500 horses on the grounds which will race at a certain distance. When the conditions state that the race is for a certain age, or for fillies and mares, or for horses bred in that state, you are narrowing down the possible entrants and consequently getting a weaker field.

Other restrictions may change the conditions of a race. It may be for non-winners of two races over a lifetime, or three races lifetime. This also weakens the caliber of the field. *Daily Racing Form* now prints the conditions of the race.

In determining the class of the horse, look at all the races listed in the past performances, not just the last few. Find out at what level the horse has been successful. If he has raced over his head since, regardless of where he has finished, and he is now back to his proper level, he may be worth a play—provided other conditions are suitable. If all of his races have been for a higher price, and he has shown a reasonable amount of speed, he should be well thought of.

Some of the things to look for in horses that are dropping down and have raced recently are: early speed against higher company; an ability to make up some ground; or an even race where he was not beaten too badly.

When a horse has raced for $4,500 and finished last, beaten 25 lengths every time, it is of course no indication that he can run for as low as $3,500. My theory is that anybody can trail the field in the Kentucky Derby.

Another aspect of racing that must be considered when distinguishing the class of the field occurs in *allowance races*. All races are not claiming races, and at some tracks allowance races predominate. How do we therefore tell the allowance races apart? I'll have to go back to the same thought again. *If* you are a regular, you should keep the charts or have a good memory.

The conditions of allowance races vary a great deal. Many allowance races are for non-winners of a certain number of races, or over a certain distance, or for a certain amount of money. When you find an allowance horse which has raced in wide-open allowance competition, with no restrictions, moving into a race for non-winners of two races lifetime, you have a large class drop.

One good thing about the allowance category is that there are not as many horses to keep track of, and when you see one which has raced against the better allowance horses on the grounds mixed with some horses not in that class, you can spot it more easily. The conditions of allowance races point out the classier races; you must know what those conditions were to be accurate about class drops.

Handicaps are usually easier to calculate than allowance races. Some horses race in handicaps almost exclusively, and *Daily Racing Form* spells out these handicaps by name. The handicap horses will usually defeat the allowance horses.

The final type of race that must be considered is the maiden race. The maiden race (for non-winners), is often very difficult to analyze. The one thing you must know is that a maiden claiming race is almost always weaker than a maiden allowance race, (listed as just "maiden") and the claiming ladder is basically the same. Because of a limited number of maidens running in low claiming races, you may find the same horses running one day for $3,500 and a week later for $5,000. Again, your memory will play a large part in telling a classier one from a lesser one.

One of the most useful sections of *Daily Racing Form* is the line listing the three finishers in their previous races. By constantly using this variable, you will soon develop a better memory for the horses' names, and it will help you immensely in determining class. I must admit, it takes great concentration and an ability to remember, but without these skills one cannot expect to be as successful as one who has them.

It must be understood that many races are not open and shut. Many allowance races, for instance, are difficult to tell apart. All the horses have faced decent competition and are capable of winning that particular race. In handicaps, the best horses in a category are entered and all have merits. In maiden races, you may have such a variety of claiming prices or maiden allowance runners that it becomes confusing. Many claiming races are filled with ten or twelve horses which have competed against the same type of opposition.

When you see these races, they are obviously the ones to skip or wager lightly on. However, when you see the one ore more races where there are horses *legitimately* dropping down, horses which have shown some run against better opposition, and have present physical fitness, these are the best plays at any racetrack. The most subtle class drops of just $1,000 in claiming price can make a good-priced winner out of a loser. You should spend a great deal of time studying the *competition* faced by horses in their previous races. If you have the opportunity to follow one circuit of racing, pay a great deal of attention to the first three finishers in previous races. You may find a horse that ran fourth last time. If, in your mind, all three which finished ahead of him would easily destroy this present field—you may have a winner.

I am a firm believer in spending most of my time in finding the answers to the two basic questions. These are: Which horses are physically fit? Which have competed on a higher level of competition?

I spend very little time poring over a myriad of times, numbers, and statistics. I believe that by statistics a user can prove anything he or she wants. I am sure I could show that a certain percentage of races are won by the number six horse on cloudy days.

Statistically, you will find that any one of hundreds of facts, when used in a certain way, will point out 33 percent winners. There must be more than taking a set of numbers and finding the highest or lowest number from twelve horses. We can all add, subtract, and multiply, so if it were that easy, we would be retired millionaires. Finding that level of competition is the key, and we will talk about how to find it in a coming chapter.

CHAPTER 4

Study the variables

The great number of factors that go into deducing a winner at the racetrack will be referred to as *variables*. There are many variables that determine the outcome of a horse race, most of which are printed in *Daily Racing Form*. Unfortunately, some are not listed anywhere and are not known by anyone until after the race. The variables at hand, however, can give you the necessary knowledge to produce a high enough percentage of winners for a profit—*if* properly interpreted.

During the following chapters I will take each variable, show you where it is located, and how to use it. The key words are *"how* to use it." A hundred handicappers may find fifty different meanings to each variable. If everyone knew exactly the importance of class as compared to time, weight compared to jockey, etc., we could all retire on our racetrack winnings. Unfortunately, the game wasn't meant to be easy. One must make his own interpretations as to the relative importance of each variable, and how it applies to each race.

I have my own theory as to which variables carry the most weight, and *I feel very strongly that I have found the secret to sound handicapping.*

We will discuss the variables to consider when making that final selection. Certain conditions in a race may not favor the best horse, but give the second-best horse an excellent chance. Things such as post position, jockey, or distance can make the best horse a dead loser.

In handicapping a race, one must learn to narrow the field down by eliminating those that cannot win, or those that are very bad risks because of a lack of ability and/or physical fitness. The next step is to take the contenders and determine which, because of race conditions, are best suited to win.

Naturally, the ideal is to end up with one horse. When your deductions narrow a field down to one horse, and if you've diagnosed correctly, you should have a good percentage of winners, enough to make a solid profit.

Remember, however, that a certain percentage of those top selections will lose because of either bad racing luck or an intangible factor that took place before the race that you were unaware of, or during the race that was unforeseen. But if you've done the job correctly, you will be rewarded with satisfaction and a good profit.

CHAPTER 5

Consider age and sex

A s we begin to define the variables that go into answering our two basic questions, and giving to each variable a value, let me say again that one hundred different handicappers will have fifty different interpretations of the importance of each variable. Herein lies the basic reason why everyone has not made a fortune playing the races. The actual value to be placed on each variable is a highly arbitrary matter; I base my opinions on not only forty years of handicapping, but the past 23 years of being a track handicapper at different racetracks.

During my years in the racing business, I have interviewed countless owners, trainers, jockeys and racing officials. From what they had to say about the racing business, and from what I already know, I believe my evaluations of the variables are as sound as one could get. They are based on every bit of available information.

Listed in the past performances of each horse in *Daily Racing Form* is the age and sex of the horse. These are found atop the actual performances of the horse, and are significant when you try to answer the questions of class and fitness.

Age

The age of a horse directly relates to the probable fitness of the animal in question. Certain things should be put into focus about the cycle of fitness in race horses.

A race horse, much like a human being, is made physically fit by exercise. The trainer works his horses out in the mornings, bring him to or near the desired physical level, then continues the process by competition. Once the horse is fit, he will stay fit for a period of time, then become tired if overraced, and show signs of physical decline. At this point, the trainer ordinarily rests the horse for a time, builds back his strength, and returns him to readiness for action in the same manner as before.

It is quite obvious that age plays a great role in the horse's fitness. A younger horse, for example, will round into shape more quickly than an older one. He will undoubtedly hold his form longer, and return from a rest more quickly. Horses reach the peak of their racing career between the ages of four and five. Some horses are very strong at the end of their 3-year-old year. Most horse people to whom I have talked say that at the age of five, the horse should be at his best. He is fully developed, has the experience, and should be at his racing peak.

It must be assumed, then, that a younger horse will need less time and training to be ready to compete. If you are handicapping a 4-year-old in a race who has been away for six months, you may expect that he can return in winning form is his training has been complete.

An older horse, on the other hand, rarely can return, after a long lay-off, in the peak of condition ready for competition.

If one would think of it terms of human beings, you wouldn't expect a 37-year-old hockey player to be sharp after returning from a three-month layoff from a fractured ankle. He may return to action, but may be a far cry from the player he was three months ago. I would say that to play a horse which has laid off for a month or more and is beyond the age of seven years would be very risky. The longer the layoff, the bigger the risk. I make it a general rule to discount the chances of *any* horse past seven that has had two or more months off.

Younger horses can also be expected to perform well for a longer period of time. If I were to see a 4-year-old run a bad race, I would think he could bounce back from it his next time. An 8-year-old, however, after a bad race, may be more likely to be on the downward trend and should be avoided.

Older horses also have more aches and pains and find it harder to campaign than the younger horses—just as with human beings. The 37-year-old hockey player may feel great one day, and be very sore the next and not perform well. The younger player would show more consistency.

The older you get, the more you slow down. Athletes who were very fast in their younger days realize they have lost a step or two in later years and a day comes when they can no longer compete at all. An $8,000 horse at age five will have a harder time competing on that level at age nine.

There are, of course, exceptions to every rule, and some older horses are like vintage wine. They can race on a competitive level with their younger counterparts nearly as well as they did earlier in their career. The classier horses will also break my rule at times, and be just as hard-hitting at nine as they were at five. In general, however, one must follow sound principles that hold up a good percentage of the time.

In answering the question of fitness in the animal, always use the age of the horse in conjunction with his workouts and recent races, along with his present form. Be much more skeptical of the older horses; take greater chances with younger horses. Stay away from older horses after long lay-offs, or when they are apparently tailing off; they may need long rests. Give some consideration to a 5-year-old making his first start of the season. Now in the peak of his racing life, he may be much improved over his last year's record.

Sex

The sex of a horse may have a lot to tell about its class. Where age may help in answering the fitness question, sex may aid in answering the class question.

After talking to many trainers and jockeys, I have found there is a great difference of opinion as to whether a filly can compete with a horse. I know trainers who would rarely race a female against a male; others do it on a regular basis with no qualms. After watching thousands of races over the past few years, I have reached some general conclusions.

1. I believe that females can compete against males with little or no problem when the racing is on a low level. The cheaper race tracks card many $3,000 claiming races. Yet few top races will find females and males mixed. Females, when fit and at the right claiming level, just as males, win their share of races.

2. As the racing gets more competitive, I find that females do not fare quite as well, perhaps due to the fact that at the bigger tracks they seldom compete against the males. In major racing, many races are carded for fillies and mares and there is little need for the trainer to run against open competition.

3. I have a tendency to stay with a male over a female in an important handicap race, but would pay no attention to the sex in a $3,500 claiming affair. Some females have raced very successfully against the males in the past. Certainly Dahlia, at her best, never took a back seat to any thoroughbred, and Ruffian had few of either sex capable of beating her. Personal Ensign also falls into this category.

In handicapping an average race at an average track, I would not preoccupy my time with which horses were females and which were males, but would spend time looking at what *type* of races they ran in. When a race is restricted to fillies and mares, *Daily Racing Form* indicates such by placing a symbol "F" with a circle around it. This indication tells you that the race was restricted.

In Chapter 3, I mentioned that any restricted race must be considered weaker than a non-restricted race at the same claiming level. Again, a $5,000 filly and mare race going six furlongs can only draw from a certain pool of horses on the grounds: only fillies and mares whose owners wish to compete at that price and at that distance. The same race, when opened up to males, may have double the amount of possible entrants, thus making it more difficult. Because you never know which of the horses in that category will enter, you can't be sure how tough the race will be. But on percentage alone, the open race would likely draw the tougher field.

In determining the class of a filly in an open race, it therefore would be wise to see if the filly had been competing primarily against female opposition. If this is the case, and the claiming price was the same or lower than the present race, it should be concluded that the past race was an easier spot than this one. Naturally, there will be times when a $5,000 filly and mare race may be tougher than the open event, but for the most part it is not. Again, we see the percentages come into play. You may eliminate a filly winner in a race and be sorry. Remember the many others you didn't play that lost.

Another way to look at this is to take a filly that has competed against the males time and time again and now drops into a filly and mare race at the same claiming level. If she had competed reasonably well with the males, she would be considered dropping into a softer spot with her own sex. It *may* not be—as claimed—that fillies can't beat males, but more likely that the open race drew stronger opponents than is available for this race.

One of the *real* drop-downs to watch for is the filly that has been coming close in, let's say, a $7,500 open race, and now moves in with $7,500 fillies and mares under similar conditions. I use the world "conditions" because that could also have a bearing on the class. For example, a filly competing against $7,500 non-winners of two races lifetime, in open competition, may be in a tougher spot when she races with $7,500 fillies and mares without restrictions. There is that fine line, at times, that determines the true class. Both races were restrictive, but the non-winner race was more so.

However, most of the time one need not nit-pick. If you play every race, or nearly every one, you can use your principles of percentages and come out okay in the long run. The player who plays only a race or two a day may want to define that small class distinction before he makes his wager. Remember, though, that any race that restricts the possible entries must be assumed to be a cheaper race at the same claiming level than an open race under most conditions. Check carefully to see that the sex is establishing and, in the case of females, what type of races they competed in. Use this to get a clearer picture of the class of the horse.

CHAPTER 6

The matter of breeding

You may now suspect that the pattern I'm following to list the variables coincides with the order in which *Daily Racing Form* prints them. When your eyes scan the horses' past performances, from top to bottom, left to right, this is the order you will see them in.

To the right of the age and sex of the horse is the horse's breeding lines. Here is where you find out the horse's sire (father), dam (mother) and sire of the dam (grandfather), along with the state in which the horse was bred.

Breeding can be used, in most cases, to aid in determining the class of the horse before he actually has established his form. In 2-year-old racing, with horses that have never started, or only started a few times, the handicapper may use the breeding lines to decide whether the horse has enough class to compete with the others.

I would first like to say that a person could be a good handicapper and know very little about breeding. It may not be unwise to forget the 2-year-old maiden races altogether in your gambling, especially those races with many first-time starters. If you really wish to learn about breeding, it will become almost a study in itself to read books and subscribe to the prominent national breeding magazines such as *The Blood-Horse*. Personally, I have not made as much a study of breeding as I would like to, but I can suggest an approach to it that avoids the burden of heavy research.

I have made it a point over the years to look at the breeding of *every* horse in *every* race. This aids you in learning the names of the better sires and dams. You may find that certain sires produce speed horses or distance horses, and it could help you in choosing a first-time starter. When I talk to people who attend the yearling sales most of them acknowledge that the dam is between 50 and 60 percent of the breeding; yet the dams, for the most part, are unknown by name to the average fan. Sires who have distinguished themselves in racing and have made names for themselves are easy to remember. Fillies and mares get far less fanfare than the males and even the good ones become unfamiliar after a few years.

To be a really good judge of breeding one must have as much knowledge of the dam's side as of the sire's side. Looking at the sire of the dam can sometimes give an indication of good breeding on both sides. For instance, a Seattle Slew colt out of a Danzig mare would have to be considered royally bred even if the dam had never raced, which is the case many times. Sires are also better known because they sire many thoroughbreds each year while a dam can foal but one a year and will have fewer in her career to be remembered by.

All of this hasn't stated enough about using breeding to answer the question of class. Let's elaborate on that aspect.

When I see a field of 2-year-olds that have raced few times, and the field has at least three first-time starters, it becomes a very difficult race to handicap. With three first-time starters, it would be impossible to determine that all three are poor. One of the three may be fast, yet you can't know it. Whenever there are unanswerable questions such as this, you can only guess as to the outcome.

If there happens to be one first-time starter in the race, or perhaps two, you may be able to make a determination. By looking at breeding, workouts, and appearance, you may feel that one of the starters is superior to the rest of those who have started, and you need only worry about the other first-time starter.

My philosophy has always been that when I see a bad field of maidens, and one or two first-time starters, I know the rest can't run, but maybe one of the newcomers can. The best time to be a first-time starter off his breeding and workouts is when the others have had their chances and have done poorly. This is usually a great spot for the first-timer. If he can run at all, he can down the field. Usually when a first-time starter catches a bad lot and has good breeding and workouts, you may have as sound a bet as any. Especially watch the odds board; if they are wagered upon heavily, they usually run well.

The state in which the horse was bred is also significant to me when determining whether the breeding is good or bad. Some states are known for their thoroughbred breeding and these produce, on the average, a better grade of animal than the others. Kentucky, for example, is about the best in the country for raising and breeding thoroughbreds. If I were looking at a fist-time starter who was foaled in Kentucky, I would be more impressed than by one foaled in Missouri where there is no pari-mutuel wagering.

The major breeding states other than Kentucky, are Florida, California, Maryland and Virginia. States such as New Jersey, Washington, Arizona, Louisiana and Texas have made great strides in recent years, but are not up to par with the top ones yet. If a horse has been bred in almost any other state, and has unrecognized parents, you have to assume the breeding may leave something to be desired. But in any case where the sire or dam is a good one, the state of birth makes little difference.

As a handicapper, I always look at the breeding lines of every horse in every race, and the state where it was foaled. In handicapping 2-year-old races I use these lines in many cases to determine my play—if any. You may use the breeding line to determine class, or the best distance at which the horse may be able to compete. As an example, in short 2-year-old races, I would prefer a son of the speedy Mr. Prospector over one of the plodding Temperance Hill.

This can also be used for 3-year-old maiden races where there are a number of first-time starters. Sometimes a horse with a few poor starts under his belt may improve dramatically at a huge price. A nicely bred horse that failed to respond in a few early starts may wake up and run to his breeding after the trainer finds some secret about him. Sticking with a horse of this kind for a few races may pay off in a healthy win mutuel.

Breeding could be written about in more detail, but I find its value to a handicapper of minor importance for the most part. A majority of races are filled with horses which have competed on a regular basis and have established their form. Once form has been established, breeding is of no value. You will see many sons of formerly great horses running throughout the country at bull rings and cheaper ovals. They are there because that's where they belong.

If one would like to make a study of breeding, it would be an interesting undertaking, but would aid the handicapper in a small percentage of races. One can do without a vast knowledge of breeding and still make money at the racetrack.

It is good to have as much knowledge of racing as possible, however, as there may be a time when you select a winner that makes you a lot of money. You need all the knowledge and any edge you can get. The difference between winning and losing over a period of time *may* be just a few races.

Perhaps your limited knowledge of breeding leads you to a first-time starter that presented you with a $50 win mutuel and a $600 exacta. When you add up those extra races you win because of a *little* more knowledge than the next guy, you will find they mean a lot to your wallet in the long run. Although breeding may not be the most important aspect of handicapping, it has its place and should not be ignored.

CHAPTER 7

The trainer is an important person

Immediately above the past performances and underneath the age and breeding line of the horse listed in *Daily Racing Form* is the name of the trainer. It is one of three names listed in the same area, but is the only one of any real importance to the actual handicapping. The *Form* also lists the owner and the breeder, neither of which are significant to the ability of the horse to run.

At times one may wish to know if the owner and breeder are one and the same, making the horse—in horse-racing parlance—a homebred. This means the horse was bred *and* is being raced by the same individual or stable. I can't see where this makes any difference, nor have I ever seen any study or statistic showing the relation of homebreeding to winning races.

The *trainer*, on the other hand, is very important to the running ability of the horse in question, and although knowing this does not directly answer the two basic questions, it has a bearing in your separation of contenders in a race.

Many handicappers pay little or no attention to the man who is—in essence—"coaching" the horse. Others may use the trainer almost exclusively in making their selections. Somewhere between lies the importance of the "coach" in training horses.

As in all walks of life, there are bad trainers and there are good ones. Some are far superior to the others in their chosen profession. The good ones are often named in the program under the category of trainer standings, and are listed in order of most wins and/or winning percentage. This is usually a very good indication of the ability of the trainer. Some good trainers are rarely listed in the standings because they don't have sufficient horses under their care to win the number of races necessary to have their names listed. Their winning percentages, however, may be high and should be considered. Others whose names are not listed, and who train a large enough stable, may not have the ability to train competently to compete with the better conditioners.

If you talk to trainers or jockeys, they like to minimize their importance to winning races. They will usually tell you that the horse does the running and that most trainers train the same way. Other people in racing, not necessarily trainers, have different views on the matter. A common remark concerning a poor trainer's ability is, "He couldn't train a dog to eat meat." This may well sum up the ability of some conditioners to handle horses.

I do not wish to demean the dedicated men who make up this fascinating sport, but one must face facts: There are good ones and bad ones, just as there are bad bus drivers and good bus drivers, bad shoe clerks and good shoe clerks. The handicapper must learn to recognize those trainers who get the most out of their stock and give the horses an edge.

My suggestion for those who are regulars at a track or a circuit of racing, where they can get familiar with the trainers and their habits, is to keep a study of trainer standings. Which trainers rarely win? Which often win? Use this information in handicapping. You cannot minimize the importance of the trainer. The leaders are there because they deserve to be. Year in and year out, they do the best job, and consequently get more horses to train from owners who are impressed with their work.

On my way from Arizona to Monmouth Park one summer, I happened to pass by Fairmont Park in Illinois. I mentioned to my wife that I knew of a nice Holiday Inn near the racetrack that had an indoor pool and play area, just right for us and the two children to spend some time relaxing after our long automobile journey. We checked in at about 1:00 p.m., and because Fairmont offers night racing, I had plenty of time to buy a *Racing Form* and lounge around the pool studying the card for that evening.

After spending three hours of looking at totally unfamiliar horses, jockeys and trainers, I had drawn some conclusions, especially about the first race. In the opening half of the daily double, I saw a horse that I loved, breaking from the number two post position. I was certain that he would be one of the long shots of the race. My only trouble was that the second race seemed nearly impossible to handicap. After three hours of grinding study, I still had six eligible contenders. Not wanting to spend too much money, I knew I had to make a decision.

Upon arriving at the track, I found my first horse to be 15-1, a juicy price to say the least. I decided I could afford no more than $12.00 in the first race. I purchased $6.00 combine on number two. That left me with another $6.00. As time was short to place my daily double wagers, I was still uncertain as to the three horses I would use with my horse in the first race. Finally, I went to the trainer and jockey standings. I noticed that the number two horse was trained by a leading trainer, one who had twice the wins of any other trainer, and the jockey was the meet's second-leading rider. He primarily rode for the leading trainer.

This was an older horse and would undoubtedly be the favorite. But from looking at his performances, he would have been one of the six I'd ordinarily throw out. There was something about his running style I did not like. Finally, confronted by the daily-double seller with his normal lack of patience, I was forced to decide on the three picks for the double. I used the horse with the leading trainer. As it turned out, my first horse won and paid better than $30.00, and the leading trainer took the second half for a $219.00 double.

The moral of this story is that if you are not in a position to know the trainers and their abilities, or you are at an unfamiliar track, use the statistics to point out the leaders and use this to decide a difficult race. The one factor helped me to win most of the cost of my cross country trip. Sometimes it is the little things that put you over the hump.

When at a track on a regular basis, learn the habits of the trainers. You should know their patterns. Some, for instance, are excellent at scoring with first-time starters, or horses that have returned after a long layoff. Some trainers will drop a horse in class, not because he is sore with hopes of having him claimed, but simply to win a purse. Other trainers run horses consistently over their heads, and even a slight drop does not guarantee any improvement.

Trainers will also get hot during a particular meeting, especially with certain kinds of horses. You should learn to recognize when a trainer has put over a long shot, and comes back soon with a similar situation.

At Lone Star Park, trainer Jim Gaston was having a great meet and most of what he did turned out right. Take the case of bottom-type Texas-bred claimer Faithful Word. He could do no better than third in a $5,000 state-bred claimer in the race from which Gaston claimed him, and even though he was competitive for $5,000, he didn't seem the type to have much potential for moving up in class. Nevertheless, Gaston won with him at first asking for $7,000, then again for $9,000.

White	Terry Longshore (Garland, TX) White, Brown Diamond Framed "G", Brown Bars on Sleeves													Jim Gaston	
2	**Faithful Word** 🏇 **(L)**								Claim Price: **$8,000**					**119** Ronald Ardoin	
5-2	Dk.B./Br.g.5 Hopeful Word-Marie of Essa by Pro Consul Breeder: Mike Tomlinson,TX (May 29, 1992)													(368-74-58-47)	
26Jun97	LS7	gd 3u	Clm10000	6¦¹	22⁸³	45⁴⁸	1:16²⁶	74	3/6	3	2ʰᵈ	2ʰᵈ	4²¦	5⁸¦	Cloninger,W	122
20Jun97	LS9	ft 3u	Clm14000	1¦₁₀	47²⁰	1:11⁹⁸	1:44⁵⁸	74	3/10	2ʰᵈ	1ʰᵈ	2ʰᵈ	5⁴¦	5⁹¦	Cloninger,W	114
06Jun97	LS7	ft 3u ⑤	Clm9000	6¦	22¹⁶	45³¹	1:10⁷⁸	89	9/13	2	6⁵¦	4¹¦	2¦	1²	Cloninger,W	112
18May97	LS10	ft 3u ⑤	Clm7000	6¦	22¹⁴	45⁴²	1:12⁵⁵	89	6/14	1	2ʰᵈ	1ʰᵈ	2¦	1¦	Cloninger,W	112
08May97	LS1	ft 3u ⑤	Clm5000-c	5¦¹	21⁸²	44⁹⁸	1:03⁹⁴	74	3/11	3	3¹	4³	3⁴	3⁴¦	Cochran,N	122
			Claimed from Mays James W., Jack T. Palmer Trainer													
18Apr97	LS1	ft 3u	Clm5000nw1/6m	6¦	22⁰⁴	44⁸⁵	1:10⁸⁰	80	1/12	5	1ʰᵈ	2¦	1ʰᵈ	1¹¦	Cochran,N	122
14Mar97	Hou2	ft 4u	Clm5000	5¦¹	22⁷⁶	46⁶³	1:05⁹⁸	75	3/7	4	2ʰᵈ	2ʰᵈ	2³	2³¦	Frazier,R	120
01Mar97	Hou10	fm 4u	Str5000	⌐5¦	22⁷¹	46²⁷	1:00³⁵	75	3/10	4	2¦	3¹¦	2¹	5²¦	Lowrance,C	117
10Nov96	RP6	ft 3u	Clm5000	6¦	22⁰⁰	45²⁰	1:10⁴⁰	75	7/12	1	1²	1ʰᵈ	3²¦	3⁵¦	Perner,E	116
05Oct96	RP5	ft 3u	Clm12500	6¦	21⁶⁰	44⁶⁰	1:10²⁰	74	12/12	1	4¹	6⁴	7⁶¦	8⁷¦	Stanton,T	116
Workouts:															

Keep your eye out for hot barns and give them extra consideration off claims, and in general.

A trainer has a big job to do in getting horses to the winner's circle. First, he must know how to prepare a horse for racing. He should have a knowledge of what brings an animal into top condition. He must also be able to work with a horse's infirmities so that the horse will be able to perform despite the minor ailments.

Next, a trainer must master the reading of the ever-important condition book. He must have his horses placed, for the most part, in races where they stand a chance to win. Although this seems elementary, many trainers fall in love with their horses and are afraid to lose them through the claiming box. These are the trainers to be very wary of. They seldom win races and do little more than fill up fields. Stick with the trainers who are obviously shrewd in spotting their horses.

Another thing necessary to train horses is intelligence. Unfortunately, not everyone has the same mental capabilities, and more intelligent people will do better than their mental inferiors.

It must be remembered, however, that no one can expect a trainer to win with an inferior horse. In handicapping, do not fail to answer the questions of *class* and *fitness*. If a horse does not qualify as capable or fit, the trainer will be of little importance. The trainer should only be used when you wish to make a distinction between two capable horses. It is a factor that can be used when you are a newcomer to the track. Also remember to look for patterns of trainer; this will spot you a nice play like

Faithful Word. It doesn't take many of those races to turn your losses into winnings.

CHAPTER 8

The dates of previous races count

W e now move into the actual past performance line of the horse. To the far left of his performance line, the first thing you see is the dates of his listed races.

Of all the things one can look at it in studying a horse's past performances, everything is secondary to the dates of his previous races. No other statistic or area of his performances should be analyzed before studying the dates of his most recent races.

That all-important question of physical fitness is, for the most part, answered here. One cannot expect an unfit horse to win a race regardless of how fast he ran last time, where he finished, or what the claiming price was. An inexperienced or careless handicapper may see that a particular horse won his last by six lengths for $6,500. Today's race is for $5,000. All the previous is immaterial if his win came three years ago. The question of fitness, which is not hard to answer, is the first step in handicapping.

The dates of the horse's recent races shouldn't be passed over lightly with a casual glance. Many times a race in March of one year has been mistaken for a race in March of the current year. During the month of March, a handicapper gets used to seeing the abbreviation for March in the lines of the past performances. Unless he takes the time to be sure it was March of the *current* year and not March of a year ago, or years past, he may be backing an animal who will be lucky to make it around the track.

Be careful of another pitfall: At times, a horse would have had one race in March of the current year, and the previous races were in March and February of the previous year. This means that he has had only one start in a year's time. This mistake can be made easily unless you *study* previous dates.

Another situation that crops up with regularity is the case of the horse that raced during the meeting, laid off for two months, then came back with a tightener. People become careless when handicapping a familiar track and tend to ignore the gaps in the previous races. One often looks at how many times the name of the track is listed beside his recent races rather than the dates. In the case of a long meeting, a horse may have raced twice in April, then laid off until September. Although when you look at it quickly you may feel as if the horse had started three times at the meeting—actually the first two were so far back that he is, in effect, starting his training all over again.

Although these examples seem elementary to the experienced handicapper, and illustrate a mistake that should never be made, I have personally seen good handicappers hastily think that the last race was recent—when it was in fact a year or more ago.

Horses that are campaigning with regularity, then suddenly take two or more months off, are often not good bets on the first time back, but make excellent wagers on the second outing.

A horse may be given a much needed rest after a hard campaign when it appeared that he was tailing off. He resumes training and makes his first start in two months and is probably not a good bet his first start back, but may make an excellent wager in his second outing. You may see a horse come on a bit to finish fourth off the layoff, which could be a useful conditioner, then wins his next start.

Another strong angle is the third start off a long layoff. If a horse was competitive at today's price or higher in the past, he may come back with a couple lack-luster efforts. If he suddenly starts showing some good works, he could be ready to stride at a big price.

Cheap horses are laid up for a purpose. Rarely does a trainer take a $5,000 horse and let him sit in the barn eating his oats unless it's necessary. As you can see, when a horse is able to, he runs often. The cheap horse is not easy to bring back after a layoff. He or she usually needs a race or two to regain past form. One thing is certain. The trainer did not rest him just to be kind.

Higher class horses, on the other hand, can be laid off for similar periods and come back as strong as before the layoff. More expensive, classier horses race less frequently and are more used to layoffs. Also, the trainer does not wish to risk injury, and usually runs his better horses only when they are fit to win. After short layoffs, as shown in the aforementioned examples, a classy horse is much more capable of returning to winning form at first asking. Longer layoffs must be treated differently. Even a good horse must be physically fit.

To expect a horse to be at his best, he must be physically fit. As a handicapper, your first and foremost question should always be: Is he fit enough to win this race?

The two basic ways to make this determination are through his past races and his latest workouts. Other than a personal relationship with a trainer which may reveal the horse has been secretly working at a nearby training track, or before the clockers were on the job—the facts are there for everyone to see.

If he has raced on a regular basis, without long breaks in his schedule, he must be considered physically fit. If he has not raced, then you must decide by his workouts whether he is fit enough to win at first asking. You may also consider the trainer aspect in making your decisions. As I mentioned in a previous chapter, some trainers can bring a horse back ready to win after a series of workouts, others cannot. After establishing which horses in a race are fit to win, you can proceed from there to further narrow down the field.

One point must be made at this time. In speaking of fitness, I do not refer to *soundness*. A horse may be physically fit, but sore enough so he is not able to run his best. Soreness is often very difficult to detect. A handicapper must assume that the veterinarians would spot a horse which is unsound. If they miss it, it wouldn't seem practical to assume that the average fan could detect it.

Trainers will tell you that most cheap horses are run regularly with infirmities—as does an athlete in mid-season. Many football players by mid-season have enough aches, pains, and discomforts to make it difficult to play at top speed. Race horses during a vigorous campaign also develop the aches and pains associated with competition. This does not mean they cannot perform well enough to win.

I believe soreness can be detected by long periods of absence from the racetrack. An example is a horse that lays up a month or more with no published workouts. Usually these animals are too sore to allow to race or work out, and the layoff takes them out of condition. When the horse recovers sufficiently to race again he is usually in *need* of a race.

Class horses race less often afflicted with infirmities. Trainers are more careful with them, and when a valuable allowance or handicap horse is run, he is generally free from any major infirmity. This is why skilled handicappers prefer to handicap the better races on the card.

All in all, unsoundness that develops without warning is the major reason why winning any large percentage of races is difficult. It is the unknown factor, the intangible, that can make a probable winner a loser.

CHAPTER 9

Look at the tracks of previous races, and number of race

L isted just to the right of the date a horse last raced is *where* he raced and in *what* race on the card he competed. Where he has been racing is a subject that takes special attention.

When a horse has been campaigning at any racetrack for a number of times, the handicapper can move on to other pertinent data. But, when a horse has recently shipped in to a new track, or it is the beginning of a meeting where all horses are coming in from elsewhere—certain principles for treating this factor should be considered.

When a horse has campaigned for a number of races at the present location, the major determination should be whether or not he likes the oval. Some horses will run very well on one track, and are very dull on another. Usually the makeup of the track itself, the soil and other characteristics of the materials in the racing surface determine a horse's preference or distaste for it. Some horses prefer a hard, fast track, others a softer, more cushiony oval.

In bad-weather climates where racing is conducted during the winter, some horses take a liking to the sandy racing surface used for snowy and rainy weather. When the scene shifts to summer racing at a track where the surface is deeper, the same horse may run very differently. It may be the other way around. Certainly, there are *horses* for *courses*—horses that perform well at some places, and poorly against similar opposition at other tracks.

In studying a horse's races at his present oval as compared to his performances before arriving, one may determine that the horse dislikes the present strip and may never run his best on it. Then again, he may run the same on both tracks.

Those who study this or are blessed with retentive memories may keep in mind the horses that perform well on a *particular* track. After a dull campaign on another oval, the horse may win early after coming back to the track he likes. Then he pays large dividends. Where there is much racing in a certain area, trainers will ship horses to another track because they feel their horse can handle the other oval better.

Another reason for a horse to enjoy one track over another is the track's layout. A speed horse may like a track which is less than a mile in circumference where, on the sharper turns with less straightaway, the closers have a more difficult time making up ground. A "closer," conversely, should do better when he moves from a half-miler to a mile track where he can get in gear on the longer straightaways.

The track at which a horse last raced may also give you a strong indication of the class of the horse. If the horse in question has been running for some time at the track you are presently handicapping, you need not pay any attention to it except for the factors I talked about in the previous paragraphs. When horses ship in from other tracks, or very early in a meeting when there are many newcomers from different ovals, one must have a knowledge of *which tracks run the better class races.*

There are major racetracks, minor racetracks, and some which are in between. To make the distinction is not always easy. Everyone can distinguish between Belmont and Penn National, but what of the difference between Penn National and Thistledown? If you are handicapping races at Philadelphia Park, you would assume a horse coming in from Belmont or Aqueduct would have a class advantage. A $25,000 race in New York would be considered better than a $25,000 race at Delaware. There are fine distinctions to be made at times, but in general a claiming race at one track can have better horses in it than a similar-priced race at another track.

If you are a regular at a particular track, or on a circuit such as Maryland or New York, you become familiar with the caliber of racing around you and understand that ship-ins from certain tracks do *not* do well at your oval—or, on the contrary, do better than before. You must make this determination from experience and past performances, and have a workable knowledge of this aspect of racing.

Looking at some of the nation's racetracks, the New York Racing Association circuit, which includes Belmont, Aqueduct and Saratoga, and the major Southern California tracks of Santa Anita, Hollywood and Del Mar, offer the best racing all year round. The Florida tracks of Calder, Hialeah and Gulfstream, during the winter months, are equal to any, along with Monmouth in the summer, and now Churchill and Keeneland. Other major racetracks just a notch below the top would be the Northern California tracks of Bay Meadows and Golden Gate Fields, Oaklawn Park, Lone Star Park at Grand Prairie, the Chicago tracks, Fairgrounds, Philadelphia, Delaware, Laurel, Pimlico and Emerald Downs, Turfway and Ellis Park. All these ovals present a high caliber of racing, and horses going from one of these tracks to another would be in approximately the same category.

Below this division would be a "between" group that does not offer major-league racing, but has highly competitive programs within which some fine horses run.

Below this will be a group of tracks considered minor racing, where most of the races are for low-class claimers; rarely to you find a decent horse campaigning there. Some tracks are upgrading the racing each year such as Turf Paradise where Arizona racing is growing each year.

Rather than spending more time elaborating on this premise, let me say that it is necessary for a handicapper to be able to tell the good tracks from the bad and be able to distinguish between those which are not obviously either good or bad.

The number of the race in which the horse performed may have little significance for the most part, but there are times when one can use this figure. Most tracks will spell out the class of the race with claiming prices and allowance races. Some lesser tracks offer a majority of low-class claiming races each day. A track that has eight $2,000 claiming races on a card, and maybe one or two allowance races, or perhaps a $2,500 race thrown in now and then, will make it difficult to distinguish between the better $2,500 platers from the poorer.

Racetracks—in general—card the better races toward the latter part of the program, with the feature usually the next-to-last race on the card, or the seventh race on a nine-race card. The sixth, seventh, and eighth races are usually for the better horses, although at the cheaper tracks all the races may be $2,500 claimers. If you were to walk into a place like Mountaineer Park, you may have a hard time picking out the class horses. The little number that tells you what race he was in may point out a horse that was in a little tougher race than another. Keeping in mind that the level of competition is so important to handicapping, this little fact could get you on a nice winner and change your day.

The daily double I hit at Fairmont Park, which I alluded to in a previous chapter, was partially decided by this very factor. My first horse was at 15-1; one of the major reasons I selected had him was because his last race came in the seventh event on the card. Although the claiming price of this race was the same as his previous one, *this* time he was in the first half of the daily double. When at an unfamiliar track, one must use any knowledge available to clear up an otherwise muddy picture. I spent much time with that race, and used every tool at my disposal. When you are a regular at a track, some of these variables are of little use, but when away from home, as we racetrackers often are, everything has a significance.

Unless you can distinguish class clearly by either your familiarity with the animals, or by claiming prices, the number of a horse's race may be of some value to you in making that determination. It is a seldom-used variable, but may come in handy some day and earn you money.

CHAPTER 10

What is the distance of a race?

When one handicaps a race and narrows the field down by eliminating those horses not fit and those that do not have the ability, a number of horses may still qualify. In continuing to narrow down a field, one of the factors used is the distance of the race.

Race horses, by their physical conformation, or training methods, usually prefer to run a certain distance. Some are very capable at both sprint distances and route races, but most of them will perform in one or the other.

A horse that is built to run fast, but does not have the equipment necessary to run a long distance, may never be able to win at anything over six furlongs. Other horses with a structure built for slow beginnings yet with long loping strides, may never be a factor at anything less than a mile. This would hold true no matter what the trainer tried to do with such a horse because his build by nature has dictated his running style.

On the other hand, a horse that is trained simply to sprint, and has never been asked to run very far, may find it difficult to go a longer route of ground. This same animal in the hands of a different trainer may be able to learn to run farther, but his present form indicates he will not.

So some run at certain distances because of conformation, some because of training techniques, but each has a running style and is at his or her best at certain distances.

Some fit and classy horses can always be eliminated from further consideration because of an unsuitable distance Some of the great horses of the past would have been beaten by inferior horses when placed at the wrong distance. This is a very common occurrence in racing: Many good horses that have laid off for some time return to competition in a sprint, although the majority of their earlier successes came in long races. Very often they are beaten by lesser animals.

In cheaper racing, horses are placed at the wrong distances on many occasions just to get them in a race. In racing, often a trainer will have a horse ready to run, but there may be no races in the condition book that will suit the particular horse. Rather than keeping him idle for a long period of time, the trainer enters the horse in a race it is eligible for, but at the wrong distance. The theory is that the race will keep him in better form than just working him out. When you see one of these badly misplaced starters, don't hesitate to eliminate him from consideration. A horse spotted at the wrong distance may be a dead loser regardless of any other single factor.

But there *are* times when one may gamble that a horse running at a wrong distance can win. Let's analyze this variable.

When a horse moves from a sprint to a long race, he will have a better chance than a horse going from a route to a sprint. A sprinter, unless hampered by poor conformation or possibly a breathing infirmity that does not allow him to run a distance of' ground, can often surprise one by winning a route race at first asking. One great advantage a sprinter has is his raw speed in relation to those who are usually used to a slower pace. A sprinter which has been asked to go all out from the starting gate many times may find himself all alone a few jumps from the starting gate among a group of horses that are usually asked to reserve themselves in the early going. Once on top, the jockey can allow the horse to settle down, and, run at a slower pace. A sprinter may find much more stamina when he's allowed to run slower in the early part of a race.

It is always dangerous for any horse to be allowed to open a comfortable lead, then slow down the pace to a point in which the lead horse is running without expending much energy. Horses allowed to run on their own, with no pressure from challenging horses, can usually run much farther and faster than ever before.

I am a firm believer that the number of challengers determines how tired the front runners get, and not how fast they run. A horse gets tired from constantly trying to pull away with rivals who are right at its side. Even though the horse may be going slowly, the jockey is usually urging it intermittently to keep up or possibly pull away.

With two horses going head-and-head in a route race, they may not tire each other out nearly as much as when three or more vie for the early lead. When a group of horses all go for the lead in a route race, regardless of' the quickness of the pace, they ordinarily all falter in the late stages.

This brings me back to the fact that when a sprinter takes an early comfortable lead, then is asked to run slower than he normally does, and is not challenged by anyone else for a long time, he can go all the way.

The best time to play a sprinter in a route race is when you find one who has shown early speed in sprints. This makes certain the fact that he has the speed to open up on routers. Even though he has quit in previous sprints, the main determination is that he will open an easy lead.

Be sure that there are no other sprinters in the race. In many routes, two or more sprinters may be entered. Usually this spells trouble for all of them, as they will challenge each other and set a pace far beyond their abilities to carry for a mile or more.

Also, take notice of a horse that has run evenly or been able to stay relatively close, then closes ground in sprints. When these horses are entered in a longer race where there is no front speed, they often can get the lead with ease because they are used to running faster in the early going. Such a horse that has shown an ability to close or maintain his speed in a sprint may be doubly tough when getting the lead in a route.

One of the prime considerations is to remember that horses fall into habits just as do human beings. When a horse is accustomed to running very fast in the early part of a race, he may find it much more to his liking when he is reserved in the early part of it and still be leading. He may figuratively say to himself: "I can run all day at this pace." And some seem to be able to do this when you least expect it.

Looking at the other aspect, a horse going from a route to a sprint is a worse play. Horses that are used to being rated out of the starting gate, and not allowed to run at faster speeds in the early parts of races, may find that the quick pace of a sprint leaves them so far behind that they can never catch up.

Do not expect a horse with early speed in route races to show early speed in sprints, unless he has sprinted before and has shown speed in sprints. Many horses are perfect for longer races.

They can cut out a moderate pace and hold it for a long distance. In a sprint, where the pace is at least a second faster, they find it impossible to keep up. when the rider tries to keep up, they ordinarily stop because they have never been asked to run that fast that early. The best chance for this type of horse is to stay as close as possible at his natural speed and hope the front runners quit and his stamina carries him past them in the late stages.

A closer in a route race seldom has much chance when placed in a sprint. Speaking in general terms, with horses placed within their racing levels, the poorest possible wager is to bet a horse with no early speed in routes, when that horse is running in a sprint.

These horses ordinarily fall hopelessly far behind and it becomes impossible to make up the ground. If the jockey tries to keep him closer than he is capable of staying, he will have no late kick. On rare occasions a horse with these past performances will win—but the percentages are so much in your favor not to play any of these plodders, that you will have saved a fortune by the time one of these losers finally makes it home first.

Speed in route races is often misinterpreted as speed in general. This is absolutely not the case. A horse that ordinarily runs in longer races and runs close-up most of the time, will rarely be on top when entered in a sprint. Closing ability in a sprint does not mean that this same horse will close in a longer race. Some closers have one run and finish it at about six- to six-and-a-half furlongs, and after that they have little left. Many horses that have shown some late speed in sprints will find themselves leading in longer races because of slower pace. Sprints and routes should be treated very differently.

I regard a "sprint" as being up to six-and-a-half furlongs. Seven- or seven-and-one-half I regard as "middle distance." A mile or over is, to me, a "route race," although in usual horse-racing terms a route race doesn't begin until at least a mile-distance. In this country, however, our racing is geared so much for sprinting that most tracks offer very little beyond a mile-and-one-sixteenth. When a track offers seven sprints daily and two one-mile races, I would consider the mile events as routes. The speed-oriented nature of racing in this country as compared to other nations makes a mile-and-a-sixteenth a very long race for most of our horses.

In summation, when a horse is racing a distance not suited to his running style, this may be enough to eliminate his chances. It also gives him a good chance when he starts next time at the proper distance. You can ignore his last race—no matter how dismal—because he raced at the wrong distance.

Sprinters can more easily adapt to running in routes when the conditions are right, meaning not much early speed in the race, and certainly no other sprinters.

Route horses are very bad plays when they are dropped into sprints unless they have shown an ability to sprint in the past. When all the races on a horse's past performances are routes, one must assume that the fast early pace of the sprint will hurt the router too much to recover. If a router is to be considered in a sprint, make sure he has shown early speed in his races so that he can at least stay close enough in the early going to rally at the end.

Closers in routes make the worse possible plays in sprints and should be eliminated in almost all cases.

CHAPTER 11

Fractional and finishing times

Daily Racing Form prints the fractional times of all races above three furlongs in their past performance lines. The fractional and finishing times are the times of the leader at each call and the winner at the finish. In calculating the actual time of a horse who was not on the lead, the rule of thumb is to deduct one-fifth of a second for each length behind. For example, if the lead horse went four furlongs in :45 seconds, and the horse you are handicapping was three lengths behind at that call, his time is assumed to be :45-3 seconds.

The use of fractional and finishing times in handicapping is one of the most arbitrary variables in horse racing. Some handicappers feel that the pace of the race determines the eventual winner and use these fractional times almost exclusively in their handicapping. Others use finishing times as the important yardstick in measuring the true ability of horses. Still others like to break down the time of the horse into quarter-miles, stating that the horse went so fast in the first quarter, the middle quarter and the final quarter. On the other hand, there are those who feel time is of little importance in handicapping, and some who use times in conjunction with other variables to arrive at a logical conclusion.

Fractional times

A major truth in horse racing is that the race is decided, for the most part, in the first portion of the race.

In a six-furlong sprint, for instance, the first two furlongs, or third of a mile, usually separates the "men" from the "boys." The good horses will run ahead or alongside the poorer horses for a while, then pull away from them when their jockeys ask for speed. A lesser animal becomes discouraged after extending himself to keep up for two furlongs, then finds it was all in vain. This usually causes the inferior animal to end up a badly beaten horse.

An analogy is if you were in a footrace with another person and as the race started you broke right with him. After running about a third of the race alongside him, with some extension of energy, you looked at your rival and saw the he was barely puffing. I'm sure that if he then decided to pull away a bit, you might lose interest and maybe even ease yourself a bit knowing you can't win.

Horses and jockeys have this same sense, and that is why a horse who finishes eighth in a ten-horse field one day against superior horses can come back with lesser ones a week later and beat them.

The question now becomes: Does the actual time of the first two or four furlongs make a difference? Can the good horse running at his own pace pull away from poorer horses when he desires?

In answering that question—a question that has been answered by many different handicappers in many different ways—I would like to say that for the most part I do *not* use fractional times. I have looked into many different methods of trying to use these times, but have found no formula that would work for a good percentage of the time. I feel I can back this statement with good common sense.

Fractional times are calculated in fifths of seconds. I hardly know what a fifth-of-a-second is. It is so short in time that it is less than a blink of an eye. Three-fifths-of-a-second is a lot to some handicappers yet it takes longer to say "three-fifths-of-a-second." Than three-fifths-of-a-second. I can't imagine a group of ten horses, breaking from different post positions, changing courses and directions, steadying, being bumped, slowing down a bit to take advantage of an opening, running wide, or any one of the many other things happening in a race, and then having three-fifths-of-a-second be the determining factor.

In human track events, where the distance may be very short and each runner must stay in a lane, and there are no turns, every tenth of a second may count. But the longer you run, and the more maneuvering you must do, the more inconsistent the time will be. My feeling is that when a $3,500 horse runs with a $5,000 horse, the latter will take the former when he so desires, regardless of the fractional time set by the cheaper horse. I have seen hundreds of races where one horse in the race had cut out faster fractions by at least three-fifths-of-a-second in his *last* race, but, even after taking the lead, was unable to hold on.

I have seen $5,000 claimers go wire-to-wire in the last race, set fractions faster than any horse he is facing in his next start—a $10,000 race—but despite getting the lead as he did the time before, he was collared early in the race by the better horses and finished back in the pack.

Class horses seem to know when they are better than a rival. I've talked to jockeys and trainers alike and almost all of them agree that horses have a certain sense of being better than certain other horses. They are not impressed when a cheaper horse opens up three lengths out of the gate. The jockey just keeps his horse close enough, and when they get to the serious running, the classier horse goes about his business and catches the lesser horse.

Can one really believe that the blink of an eyelash is the difference between two horses? Or believe if one horse raced for $3,500 in his last time out and went six furlongs in :22-2, :45-1 and 1:10-3, that he would defeat a $5,000 horse who went his last in :22-4, :45-4, 1:11? Can less than a blink of an eyelash be a determining factor in handicapping?

I think not.

If this held up enough times to make a lot of money, we would all be rich. Anyone can tell that 1:10-3 is faster than 1:11. How nice it would be if all that was needed was to make these simple calculations. Unfortunately, there is much more to handicapping than running times.

I do, however, use fractional times *on certain occasions.* When I see a horse drooping down slightly in class, who might have been asked to press a very fast pace, yet faltered from his efforts, and is now in a spot where he can get a comfortable lead—he is worth considering.

A classy horse may have battled for the early lead which went in :21-4 and :44-4, but tired and finished last with a finishing time much slower than his rivals. On this occasion, with a slight class drop, he may be able to open an easy lead and win going away, finishing much faster than his last losing effort. I am much more inclined to pay attention to fast fractions set by a horse *dropping down* than by one *moving up,* although sometimes those rising in class also repeat a win.

In calculating the pace of the race, I believe one should be more concerned with how many horses will vie for the early lead, rather than how fast they will go. A horse seems to tire much more when being repeatedly challenged by a rival, or rivals, than when he runs on his own.

A horse on the lead by himself may go four furlongs in :44-3 and still have enough to last. The next time he battles three others for the lead in a race that goes in :45-1 and he falters badly. In races where more than two horses are fighting for the lead, the jockey must intermittently urge his horse to either keep up, or pull away. You will see one horse edge away, the others come back on even terms, then another inch ahead, and the rest move back with them.

Even though they may not be cutting out fast fractions, the intermittent urging by the jockey is using up much of the horse's energy. Whenever you can be sure that more than two horses will battle for the lead, it is a safe bet that some horse will come from off the pace to win. When only two go for the lead, it is much more possible for the two front runners, especially if they get far enough ahead to run one-two. If the front runners in question are notorious quitters, I would eliminate both of them, expecting them to use each other up.

In trying to analyze how a race will be run, where each horse will be placed at different calls of the race, I am much more inclined to study the horses' running styles rather than how fast they have been in previous efforts. I ask again: Can you really believe that a time as short as a fifth-of-a-second will be the determining factor in a horse race? I personally can't. I prefer to delve into the many other variables to pick my horses, especially after losing with horses having fast fractional and finishing times.

Finishing time

I firmly believe that finishing time plays little or no role in calculating a horse's possible performance in an upcoming race. There are many other variables involved in the finishing time of a race other than how fast a horse can run.

One major factor in finishing time is *the condition of the track.* Most racetracks have an ever-changing surface, not just from day to day, but often from race to race. A track which is listed as fast for an entire week may actually have had many different aspects. One major track spent each Tuesday, which was a dark day, shifting the soil around. The track superintendent stated that as the week progressed, a great deal of topsoil moved to the inner rail and settled, causing the rail to be deeper. In the early part of the week, especially on Wednesday, the rail was at its fastest. Can you imagine trying to determine if a 1:11 on Monday in the eighth race is different than a 1:11-3 in Wednesday's seventh event? How could one know the exact condition of the track during that particular race, and knowing how swiftly fifths of a second roll by, how much slower or faster will the horse actually run?

Consider also the many things that occur during a race. A horse forced wide in heading for home may lose a full second. One that is forced to steady at a crucial point in the race may lose fifths of a second. The question is: Did they all run the same distance?

With different post positions and no specified lanes, it is impossible to believe that all ran equally far when the farther removed from the inner rail your horse is, the longer he must run.

When horses are asked to run a circumference of one mile, those closest to the rail will run a shorter distance than those farther out. Even if the track is banked, horses can lose plenty of ground when asked to run very wide on the turns. Any jockey will tell you that the shortest way home is on the rail, and that's where they try to get in most instances.

It is true, however, that some tracks have a deeper cushion along the rail, and it is not beneficial to stay closest to the inside. Each track may have its own bias, which will be discussed in a later chapter, but in general, it is a disadvantage to race wide in horse racing.

With all the factors known about how finishing time can be misleading, one cannot believe that it can be of much use in handicapping unless there is a large discrepancy between one horse and the rest of the field, and usually that discrepancy is borne out by the *class* in which the animal has been competing.

When using fractional times, be sure that there is enough of a difference in times to *really* be a factor. With no more than two-fifths-of-a-second difference between horses, one can say that they are all capable of competing in this particular race and that the fractional times will not interfere with any horse's chances of winning. In the races where there is a *large* discrepancy from one horse to the rest of the field, you should determine whether or not he is capable of defeating the class of horses he is facing that day.

A horse moving up with fast fractions may or may not be a good bet. One dropping down under the same circumstances may be an excellent play. Fractional times should not be used as the major aspect of handicapping, but rather in conjunction with other variables that help in piecing together the puzzle.

Finishing time is determined by so many things, including the pace of the race, that it is rarely a valuable tool in handicapping.

The finishing time of a horse in four different races at the same distance may show four different figures that vary as much as a second apart. Be extremely careful not to choose one horse over another simply because he ran faster in a previous race. Because of conditions, the seeming loser might have actually run faster.

Fitness and class are still what we are searching for, and unless time points out that a horse is classier or fitter than another, it should be used sparingly. Remember again, if finishing time pointed out a good percentage of winners, we would all be wealthy because anybody can see when one horse ran faster than another.

CHAPTER 12

Examine the track conditions

Themhe condition of the racetrack on a horse's past performances may have a lot to say about his chances in an upcoming race. Track conditions vary a great deal, and are listed in *Daily Racing Form*. Tracks may be "fast," "good," "slow," "sloppy," "wet fast," "heavy," "muddy," or "frozen." If it rains hard and the track becomes wet with puddles, but the undersurface remains hard, the track is sloppy. When the water sinks in, it turns the track to mud. When it begins to dry, at times it becomes heavy. It may even go to slow, in which case there is no water on the track. Before it returns to fast it may be labeled as good, which is not far from being fast, but can still slow the times.

On turf courses, track conditions are also of some importance. A turf course can be "firm," which is the same as fast, "hard," "yielding," or "soft" after rains.

The important point to remember is that many horses will not perform up to par when the racing surface becomes wet or waterlogged, and others will perform better under such conditions. Some will perform equally well on either fast or wet ovals. It must be clearly understood that many horses cannot tolerate off going and will run much below their capabilities. In speaking to many trainers and jockeys, they all agree that some run much better than usual, or at least no worse than usual, in the off going.

There may be a number of reasons for the horses' reactions to the water or mud. Trainers have told me that the conformation of their feet may determine their ability to run on off tracks. Some horses have feet shaped in such a way that mud or water causes them discomfort. Other horses relish the going because it feels good to them, or possible because of soreness that is eased by the soft track.

Individual preference, usually without reason, may also have to do with a horse's performance in off going. I know that I dislike dirt on my hands. For many years I have avoided yard work because of this idiosyncrasy. Horses are just like humans—they have likes and dislikes that are unexplainable. Some horses may enjoy the feeling of mud or water on their feet, others may dislike it and refuse to extend themselves in it.

Regardless of reason, it is obvious that some horses run poorly in the mud while others do well in it. This fact should be kept in mind. It might be a bona fide excuse for losing previous races.

Betting on "off" tracks is very hazardous because of an intangible and unknown variable that can in itself stop a horse from winning, or make a winner out of a loser. When studying the past performances of a horse on a muddy day, you should look for definite signs that the horse will perform in the mud, or that he will not perform in the mud. Having an insight into his ability in such going comes from three things.

First, if you are a regular at a track and are very familiar with the horses from years past, you may know of some who move up dramatically in the mud. A person who has seen a certain horse win in mud during past years may have a decided edge when that horse appears on a muddy day. Regulars at racetracks can win serious money when they can spot a proven mud performer.

Second, you can read in past performances. If in a horse's past performances it shows a definite sign that the horse moves up in mud—this usually shows by a number of bad races on a fast track, and sudden improvements on off tracks—you can assume that he prefers off going. On the other hand, if past performances show a definite dislike for mud—by a series of good races, then two or more bad races in off going—one might assume he dislikes the going and will run poorly.

One of the most difficult things about off going is that it is rarely cut-and-dried. It is always difficult to be sure, through past performances alone, whether he likes it or not. Most past performances do not go back far enough for you to have sufficient cases on which to base your decision. The best way is to know the horse from the past through personal experience; then you can be sure. Unfortunately, not everyone has the opportunity to get to know the horses at a particular track. And there are many new horses running at a track each season; you have no idea how they will perform in mud.

Third, you may spot a mud runner by breeding. This is the least reliable because not all offspring of a noted mud sire or dam will run effectively in the off going. This makes it a guess, which is always dangerous.

Handicapping on off tracks has an added variable that makes it nearly impossible to expect to win with regularity. Many things can happen to a horse in the mud that would cause him to lose, when he might have won on a fast track.

Horses coming from behind, for example, will have mud kicked back at them. They often get hit in the eye with mud, and besides the pain, lose their vision and will not run. They also get covered with mud, adding extra weight to the horse and rider. The slippery surface likewise makes it hard to rally. Horses that reach the lead may maintain their advantage more easily because of the difficulty in gaining traction for the closers.

There are also different kinds of mud. A horse will run poorly on one type of off track, and better on another type. This makes predicting their performances more difficult. You may lay off a horse who appears the best because he ran poorly in his last race in the mud. Then he turns around and wins his next start. He may have not run well last time because of the mud in his face, or because he just didn't care for the particular mud on that day. As you can see, the unknown factor of off tracks, which can make or break a horse on a given day, makes such handicapping very difficult.

Thus, it is very advantageous to be near the lead in off going. I find that a great percentage of winners on an off track go wire to wire. Most people who have studied the statistics on that subject have found the same result. Front runners do very well in the slop, that is when the track is covered with water but is still firm underneath. The running style of a front runner tends to allow him to skip over the puddles. The abundance of water being thrown back and the slick footing also make it difficult to make up ground. Naturally, as in all aspects of racing, you will find exceptions to this rule. You may be doing well sticking to front runners when suddenly two races are won by horses coming from well out of it.

This should not dampen your spirits, however. Percentage-wise, front runners will still do well in off going. Those horses who must close from dead last are to be ignored. It is one thing to close from fifth place, but to have to come from the end of the pack is very difficult on wet surfaces. I throw out any horse that ordinarily trails the field or runs far back of the pack when the track is wet.

When the surface is heavy or slow, closers have a much better chance. A tiring track will usually benefit the horses with more stamina. A quitter, therefore, may quit more quickly when asked to run in heavy going. The best thing to do when the surface is off is to check the first few races for any biases. If you see that one type or the other seems to have an advantage, stick with them throughout the card. Remember, you won't win every race this way because invariably some closer you least expect will win a race in the mud, but percentages remain in your favor.

Handicapping on off tracks is hazardous, to say the least, because of unknown variables. You should try to determine which horses, through their past performances or your memory, can or cannot run in off going. If there is no cut-and-dried answer, you must proceed as if the track were fast.

Early in the program, try to spot the track bias, if any. Does the track seem to favor closers or front runners, horses running on the inside or outside? If you can determine a definite track bias, stick with it for the remainder of the day. This seems to be your best bet. Front runners in general are better bets in mud or slop than closers. On heavy or slow tracks, it is necessary to distinguish the track bias.

In turf racing, usually a certain turf course will have a standing bias as to whether front runners or closers do well on soft or yielding surfaces. Soft courses are usually tiring, but the footing is not good and the closers have a difficult time. Again, decide if there is a bias and proceed from there. If there is no definite bias—to your knowledge—play the race as if it were firm.

One thing always to remember is that horses which run poorly in a mud race, or any off going race, can be given an excuse when studying past performances for the horse's next start. If a horse has had two miserable performances in a row, both on off tracks, you can ignore those races and go back to previous starts. Many long shots are picked by this very method. A horse may have had as many as four or five poor performances on off tracks, then win when the track is fast.

Remember that many things can happen to a horse during a race on a wet track. Even if the horse is a proven mud runner, something we don't know about may have happened to him to cause him to perform poorly. Do not be afraid to eliminate all off track races from a horse's past performances when he is back on the fast track. If his fast track races, no matter how far back they go, were good enough to win this one, you may have a good longshot selection.

CHAPTER 13

Odds of previous races

One of the variables to consider when handicapping is the odds at which the horse went off in his previous races. Although this variable is used to a lesser degree, it is printed in *Daily Racing Form* and should not be entirely overlooked.

To what degree a horse was regarded in his previous races may give some indication of his ability. For a person at a strange track, who doesn't know the horses, it may offer insight into the public's opinion of the horse.

An example of this is when a horse has been sent off at long odds time and time again. It is difficult to believe that a horse that is 30-1 or more in most of his previous races has much run in him, unless he is taking a distinct class drop. When I see something I like about a horse that has been beaten rather badly in previous races at approximately the same level, I like to peruse the betting patterns on the horse. If I see that he was rarely played—and I don't know anything about the horses at a strange track—I reexamine my handicapping to make sure that I have not read into his performances something that is not there in hopes of landing a longshot winner. And, when I'm not familiar with the horses and find that the public, which presumably frequented the track and had a better line on the horses, had been sending the animal in question off at long odds—I must conclude it was for a good reason. To reiterate: If you are a regular at a track it is easier to spot horses at long odds that actually have a chance of winning.

The opposite side of the picture is to take interest in a horse that has been regularly bet by the local patrons. A horse which has had action in the past was backed because many people thought he would win. This factor is not to be overlooked because a horse that has been well backed in past races may have encountered bad luck in losing some races. Just when the public has had enough of the horse, he is sent off at longer odds and wins. As a regular at certain tracks, I know this has happened many times.

After following a horse for two or three races, and playing him when he seemed most likely to win, at shorter odds, he seemed to win just when I excluded him—and would have paid large dividends. This is surely one of the more exasperating occurrences in one's horse-playing life.

I am not one to spend a lot of time watching the totalisator board, then running to the window when I see changes. But the odds can sometimes point out future winners.

When looking at the tote board, try to spot irregularities and make a mental or written note of it. For example, suppose a horse is heavily wagered upon at some point in the betting, then levels off to a normal trend. The next time the horse runs, if he failed to win his last race, you may remember that he received an unusual amount of money all at once. This is especially important early in the betting. If a horse that should be 15-1 opens up at 3-1, and stays for a time, then loses, I find that he may come back next time and win at longer odds.

My interpretation of this is that his connections may have felt the horse was ready and so bet their money on him. Often, bad racing luck may have caused him to run poorly. Even his connections may back off a bit on him next time, but he may be just as ready to win and, with the right luck, does so and pays a big price.

I am a handicapper and I rarely play a horse because he is heavily wagered upon *unless* he is a first-time starter. I like to win or lose on my own handicapping and not on someone else's selections. However, as part of my handicapping, I will make mental notes of these occurrences and use them in future races.

Look for horses that went off at high odds in a number of races, then suddenly—against the same competition—were bet down much more than they should have been, and lost. Again, there are many reasons for a horse to lose. He may come back next time and run the way bettors thought he would run the time before.

Beaten favorites are also horses to watch in future starts. Often a horse is sent off as a favorite and does not run his best race for various reasons. The next time, against primarily the same opposition, he is sent off at much longer odds—thanks to his poor performance the time before—and wins.

Horses do not run the same every out. This is especially true of cheaper horses. You may have to ignore a bad race or two without any apparent excuse. But if you have the patience to stay with the horse for a race or two more—after the public has forgotten about him—you may have a solid horse at longshot odds. That is what everyone looks for in racing.

This variable may not determine many of your wagers during a meeting. But it is there, and on occasions may help to clear up the picture. If you get hot on a horse, his previous odds may be the extra fuel you need to be convinced he can win.

Knowledge and application of the *minor* variables may give you those extra few winners that turn a losing season into a winning one. Always keep in mind: Have as many tools in your kit as you can get, and some day you may need that tool and you will make use of it—much to your profit.

Odds of previous races can also aid you in distinguishing class. A horse that was sent off at short odds against stronger competition may show you his potential. Horses that ship into a track may be difficult to assess at first. Checking on odds at a horse's previous track, especially if the track is similar in class to the one in use, may give you insight as to how well regarded he was at the other oval.

When a number of horses ship in to a track, you may get a better line on them when comparing races at their previous track. If you can see that horse "A" was sent off at lower odds than horse "B" in a race at their previous track, it may be just enough to convince you that "A" is better than "B" and should be your wager when they meet.

Always be aware of what the public's opinion of a horse is when handicapping at a strange track. Even though you should go by your own handicapping of the horse's ability, what his previous odds were may aid you in assessing his class.

CHAPTER 14

How much weight?

W e now come to a variable that is more often used and misused than any other variable. Some handicappers either eliminate horses, or wager upon horses solely because of the weight they are carrying or because of the shift in weights from previous races.

The knowledge I possess about this factor has been accumulated through my own experiences, added to what I learned from countless interviews with trainers and jockeys regarding the importance of weight. In putting the views of horsemen together with my own observations, I have come to some conclusions that I feel are accurate and worthwhile.

When is weight important?

Weight seems to be of greater importance in races run over a longer distance. Almost every jockey I've ever talked to has maintained that the longer the race, the greater is the toll taken on heavily weighted horses. When speaking of longer races, I refer to races of at least a mile. The farther they go, the more weight becomes a factor.

One of the most difficult questions to answer is: How much will weight affect any horse's chance of winning? Many handicappers apply a formula to weight, such as one length per pound, but I feel that this is absurd. I can't in any way justify a numerical value placed on weight as regards effect in lengths during a particular race. All trainers will tell that some horses are better weight carriers than others. Some will run as well with 120 pounds as they did with 115 at nearly any distance. Others are less capable of handling weight and more readily show the effects of it.

One point I would like to bring out is that weight carried by a horse below 120 pounds is of very little consequence. Conditions of races cause a horse's carried weight to fluctuate a great deal, carrying 110 one day, 115 another, and 120 another. I have found that they seem to handle one about as well as another.

Weight *can* be very important when a horse is asked to carry over 120 pounds. Weight can stop a freight train eventually, and when enough weight is put on a horse, it will also stop him. The actual point at which he will not be able to do his best is hard to tell until he carried it and failed.

I have seen many horses run with 122 pounds and run well. They will do likewise with 123 and 124. Then, when asked to carry 125, they run poorly. It is similar to lifting weights. You can continue to lift, although it becomes increasingly more difficult—up to a certain weight. When that extra pound or two is added, you can no longer lift it. A field goal kicker may be dead accurate from 45 yards, but when asked to kick 47 yards he is a total failure. There comes a point when the athlete has been tested to his maximum and cannot perform beyond that without a great deal of additional training. Even then, he may never have the physical ability to achieve the added strength.

In handicapping, one must make a determination whether the excess weight will be too much for a particular horse or not. I have made a general rule that when a horse is asked to carry 122 pounds or more for the first time in his career, over a distance of one mile or more, I usually eliminate him unless he is far superior in ability to the rest of the field.

Another time when weight may be of prime importance is in handicap competition where the weights are assigned by the racing secretary and handicapper. When handicap horses meet a number of times during a meeting, the handicapper will fluctuate the weights according to their performances in recent races. A shift in weights is what the bettor should be aware of. When one handicap horse beats another horse by one length, and next time the pair have a five-pound shift in weights, it may make a big difference in their following meeting. Usually the handicap horses are consistent and are of relatively equal ability. At equal weights, a certain horse may win a majority of the time, but when he is heavily burdened as compared to his nearest rivals, he may be unable to win. A slight shift in weights my make a difference, and should be used as an important handicapping tool.

A weight shift may also be of importance when a horse was asked to carry over 120 pounds in his last race, being asked for the first time to carry that much, then drops the excess weight for his next start. If the horse had been performing well with 117 going one-mile-and-one-sixteenth, then fails miserably with the 122 pounds against the same opposition, he may be an excellent wager when dropping back to 117, or even 119—given similar opposition.

The subtleties of weight changes are only important when it is an obvious difference. A horse that won with 114 last time out, facing the same opposition with 117 the next time, will undoubtedly not be affected by the extra three pounds. If a horse is fit and going well at the time, the few pounds added for a race, as long as it doesn't exceed your estimated limit of the animal, should be ignored.

Many handicappers have lost excellent opportunities to win because they would not play a fit horse because of a few pounds of weight.

When weight is not a factor

All of my experiences in racing, and my interviews with horsemen, lead me to believe firmly that weight is of little importance when sprinting. At races from seven furlongs and shorter, the fluctuation of weights among the horses should be totally ignored, except in handicap competition where a weight shift may rule out the top contenders. In 99 percent of the sprints run at an average track, the weight carried by horses is of little importance.

Let's qualify that. I also believe that there is a limit beyond which no horse will succeed—even in a sprint. A few jockeys have told me that when a horse is heavily weighted in a sprint, say with 125 pounds, he may tend to break more slowly. It takes him just a bit longer to get that weight moving and in a sprint it may cost him the race.

This attitude may shock many handicappers who have been so weight conscious in the past. I, too, spent many years wondering if a horse who carried 113 pounds going six furlongs would be able to go as fast with 117. I also found a great deal of frustration when I eliminated logical horses because of a few pounds of weight and then watched one of them win easily. I am a much happier handicapper now because I almost ignore weight. I am much more interested in the horse's present physical condition and his class. If he's fit, has the class, and appears well spotted, I don't even look at the weight unless it violates my rule of excessive weight. Fortunately, I rarely have to contend with it because most races have weight assignments of 120 pounds or less for all entrants. The only ones I must deal with are the handicaps and the rare races in which the assigned weights are over 120.

The most difficult aspect of using weights in handicapping is trying to evaluate each pound in relation to how fast a horse will run. I believe this to be an impossible thing to do with any accuracy, knowing that different horses handle weight differently, and that a few pounds one way or the other is rarely felt by the horse.

Deadweight compared to live weight

I have heard many handicappers ask the question about the difference between deadweight and live weight. Because I have been asked that question in interview shows at both Monmouth Park and Turf Paradise, I thought I would include it in this chapter.

One day while conducting an interview show with a jockey at Turf Paradise, a fan asked the jockey for his opinion regarding the difference between live and deadweight.

Before the jockey could give his answer, the fan vociferously pointed out that the program did not list the weight of the jockey as well as the total weight carried by the horse. Because of this, he had no way of knowing how much deadweight the horse was carrying. The deadweight, of course, is the difference between the jockey's weight and the actual weight assigned to the horse. This is made up in lead weights added to the saddle.

The jockey laughed. I believe his laughter was as good an answer as can be given.

"Bill Shoemaker," he said, "was one of the lightest jockeys to ever ride and one of the greatest. Shoemaker's horses always had to carry more deadweight than most horses in every race he rode."

Can you imagine trying to calculate, not only the horse's ability to carry the assigned weight, but also to try to determine if the deadweight he carried would slow him down more than his opponents? It is senseless to try to answer unanswerable questions, and time spent on it is simply wasted. Weight is weight, and the horse is not affected by the liveness or deadness of it.

Overweights

Another factor that many handicappers consider is the announced overweights for each race. This means that the jockey actually weighs more than the horse's assigned weight.

I had a man tell me once that he found that horses with announced overweights lost a greater percentage of the time than normal. How he obtained this statistic is not known, but there is absolutely no correlation between a jockey weighing more than the assigned weight and performance in the race. At many tracks, the leading riders are a bit heavier than they would like to be. They often ride overweight on every mount. Under the misapprehension that this makes a difference, the leading rider would not be a play in the majority of his mounts. The question then becomes: How did he get to be the leading rider with this damaging statistic against him?

I spent one summer at Longacres Race Track in Washington where two of the leading riders weighed 119 and 120. *Every mount they had was an overweight. But eliminating them from each race would certainly have hurt the players' chances to win.*

In summation, weight over 120 pounds going a distance of ground may be a factor. Weight may also be a factor in handicaps where weight shifts favor a horse that lost by a relatively narrow margin last time and faces the same type of opposition. Weight may likewise be a factor when it exceeds the horse's physical capabilities of handling it.

Most races that the average handicapper works will *not* be affected by any of the above factors. The most common one may be the horse in a route carrying over 120 pounds. But weight may be a factor at the start of a sprint when the horse is heavily burdened.

On the other hand, weight is no factor in sprints when no horse carries over 122 pounds. Weight shifts involving weights of under 120 pounds are of little or no importance at any distance except in rare cases. At times, one may find a horse that carried 120 pounds in his last race and, because of an apprentice rider and conditions, he is asked to carry 105 or so. This drastic change might be a factor, but doesn't come up very often.

For the most part, the majority of races are decided with weight being of *no* factor and a handicapper should not preoccupy himself with this. There is no difference between deadweight and live weight, and announced overweights have no bearing on the outcome of the race.

CHAPTER 15

Running style and past finishes

The meat and potatoes of actual past performances are in the horse's past finishes and how he got there. *Daily Racing Form* charts the progress of each horse during the race, showing where the horse was at different points through the finish of the race.

Although the finish is naturally important, *how* he goes about getting to the finish may be of great importance in handicapping his next race.

Every handicapper should be able to determine the running style of each horse in every race. Nearly every horse that runs has his own style, whether it's going to the lead, or coming from far back, or possibly staying close throughout the race and then attempting to wear down the leaders.

Some horses are far more versatile than others and are capable of running any kind of a race depending on the circumstances. Class horses have that ability to a greater degree than cheap horses. A cheaper horse ordinarily will run well *only* when he is allowed to run his own style of race, and where his style is conducive to winning.

Once a horse establishes a running style or shows that he has a preference in running, it is not easy to change this. A horse does best doing what he becomes used to doing. If he is asked to change that style he frequently finds the difference too much to cope with.

Let's look at the different running styles of horses. The front runner has a common style. It is often eye-catching. A front runner is a horse that attempts to break on top in each race and go wire-to-wire. Rarely does a true front runner come from behind and win. Ordinarily, when he fails to get the lead, he runs far back in the pack.

In studying the past performances of a horse in order to determine his running style, it must be understood that one race does not determine a style. You must make your determination by studying every race shown on the past performances.

You may find that he has some exceptions in his form. For example, an even-running horse may break to the lead in a particular race where there is no early speed and go wire-to-wire, or press the pace all the way. Unless the horse shows that he goes for the lead *every* time, he is not a true front runner. At times, a horse will break badly and then close ground, when all his other races show that he runs to the front end each time. The single closing race is not to be misconstrued as his being a closing horse, or even one that can successfully come from off the pace. You must determine what he will do in *this particular race*, and he will probably run the way he has run the majority of times. Let us look at a true front runner. (See chart of Groovy Add Vice).

Orange

7

5-2

Leanna L. Reidy (Houston,, TX)
Blue, Blue "K" on Silver Star, Silver Stars on Sleeves

Groovy Add Vice (L)

Ch.g.6 Groovy-Regal Taheka by Vice Regent
Breeder: Loradale & Racing InvestmentCorp,KY (March 13, 1991)

Claim Price: **$15,000**

Dallas Keen

122 E. J. Perrodin
(130-25-16-10)

03Jul97	LS7	ft	3u	Clm15000	$1\frac{1}{16}$	$:45^{57}$	$1:09^{88}$	$1:43^{88}$	**89**	5/9	$1^{4\frac{1}{2}}$	1^{7}	$1^{5\frac{1}{2}}$	1^{7}	1^{2}	Perrodin,E	116	L
13Jun97	LS7	fm	3u	Clm25000	ⓣ$1\frac{1}{8}$	$:46^{93}$	$1:10^{36}$	$1:46^{43}$	**79**	5/8	1^{1}	$1^{2\frac{1}{2}}$	$2_{\frac{1}{2}}$	$5^{5\frac{1}{2}}$	6^{10}	Perrodin,E	117	L
26May97	LS1	fm	3u	Shp10000	ⓣ$1\frac{3}{8}$	$:48^{24}$	$1:38^{50}$	$2:15^{21}$	**80**	3/9	1^{3}	$1^{2\frac{1}{2}}$	$1_{\frac{1}{2}}$	5^{5}	$6^{9\frac{1}{4}}$	Perrodin,E	113	L
10May97	LS7	ft	3u	Clm45000	6f	$:22^{20}$	$:44^{43}$	$1:08^{55}$	**78**	6/6	5	$6^{8\frac{1}{2}}$	6^{10}	$6^{11\frac{1}{2}}$	$6^{17\frac{1}{4}}$	Perrodin,E	110	L
05Jan97	SA3	my	4u	Clm45000	1	$:47^{18}$	$1:11^{74}$	$1:37^{61}$	**82**	2/7	2^{1}	3^{1}	$5^{1\frac{3}{4}}$	5^{3}	$4^{9\frac{1}{2}}$	Pedroza,M	114	BL
11Dec96	Hol1	sy	3u	Clm25000	$1\frac{1}{16}$	$:47^{05}$	$1:10^{91}$	$1:44^{13}$	**85**	6/6	2^{1}	3^{1}	3^{2}	3^{2}	1^{1}	Pedroza,M	116	BL
03Nov96	SA9	ft	3u	Clm25000	1	$:47^{24}$	$1:11^{18}$	$1:36^{01}$	**87**	5/7	1^{1}	$1_{\frac{1}{2}}$	2^{hd}	2^{hd}	$3^{3\frac{1}{2}}$	Pedroza,M	116	BL
05Oct96	SA1	ft	3u	Clm16000	1	$:46^{35}$	$1:10^{91}$	$1:37^{01}$	**87**	8/9	1^{1}	1^{1}	1^{hd}	1^{1}	$1^{1\frac{1}{4}}$	Pedroza,M	117	BL
22Sep96	Fpx9	ft	3u	Clm16000	$6\frac{1}{2}$f	$:21^{97}$	$:45^{20}$	$1:17^{11}$	**77**	2/10	6	5^{3}	$3^{2\frac{1}{2}}$	10^{7}	9^{7}	Hunter,M	116	BL
09Sep96	Dmr5	ft	3u	Clm10000-c	1	$:45^{96}$	$1:11^{09}$	$1:37^{43}$	**85**	3/10	$1^{1\frac{1}{2}}$	1^{3}	1^{4}	1^{3}	$1^{3\frac{1}{2}}$	Hunter,M	117	BL

Claimed from Anson, Ronald and Susie, Douglas R. Peterson Trainer

Workouts: ● 14Jul LS 4 ft :47.00 h 1/8 29Jun LS 4 ft :47.40 h 4/25 06Jun LS 5 ft 1:01.20 b 3/19

On only a few occasions in the past ten tries did Groovy Add Vice fail to break on top. On all but one of those occasions, he did not finish in the money. Groovy Add Vice has shown practically no ability to be rated and come from off the pace, although he is exceptionally dangerous when allowed to open up without opposition. When handicapping a true front runner, your task is to be sure that he will not be used up trying to battle other horses for the lead, and you must be certain he can *get* the lead.

Groovy Add Vice's ability to win seems to depend almost solely on how easily he can get to the front. If you have determined he will make the lead easily, you have a very solid play.

Another running style would belong to the horse that seldom takes the lead, but prefers instead to run just off the early pace. This horse doesn't have the speed to take a lead and go wire-to-wire unless there is very little speed in the race and he can get the lead without being used too much.

This is the type of horse that at times will show in front, but is not truly a front runner. This horse fits very well when he can lay just behind two or more horses that battle for the early lead. He has the speed to be close, and the staying power to take advantage of the speed duel on the front end.

This horse is rarely comfortable when he gets too far behind. At times a bad post position will force the horse to lose much ground trying to stay in contention, and he will use up his mild closing ability trying to keep up while losing ground. This type of horse is also capable of running both short and long races. He has the speed to take the lead in longer races, and at times, hold on. In shorter races, he has the ability to pass horses in the stretch. A good example of this kind of horse is Darla's Charge. (See chart).

You will notice that his best efforts are when he can lay third or fourth, but close to the pace. On a few occasions, when falling back to fifth or

White	Robert F. McCaslin (Ft Worth, TX) Black, Red "M"												Dallas Keen	
2 **5-2**	**Darla's Charge (L)** B.g.10 Ragtime Band-Miss Kinetic by Three Bagger Breeder: Churn Thoroughbred Farm, Inc.,NE (April 15, 1987)					Claim Price: $25,000						**116 Todd Glasser** (128-35-20-10)		
28Jun97	LS7 ft 3u	Clm20000-c	6f	21 87	:44 80	1:09 62	92	8/8	3	5 4	3 1	2 hd	•3 2 1/2	Ardoin,R	116
	Claimed from Nix, Jerry B. and Cart, Jerry D., Jerry D. Cart Trainer														
14Jun97	LS7 ft 3u	Clm25000	6f	22 47	:45 04	1:09 27	89	2/9	4	6 1 1/2	4 3	2 4	2 6	Ardoin,R	116
26May97	LS8 ft 3u	Clm25000	6f	22 18	:44 84	1:10 05	92	3/9	5	4 1 1/4	4 2 1/2	3 1	2 1/2	Ardoin,R	116
15May97	LS7 gd 3u	Clm25000	5 1/2f	22 01	:44 79	1:03 32	96	5/11	3	5 4	5 4 1/4	3 2	2 nk	Ardoin,R	116
20Apr97	LS6 ft 3u	Clm40000	7f	22 04	:43 99	1:21 70	87	5/10	5	3 2	3 1 1/2	3 2 1/2	3 6	Ardoin,R	116
10Apr97	OP6 ft 4u	Clm40000	6f	21 69	:45 01	1:09 62	81	5/8	5	6 6	6 5	6 8	8 9	Borel,C	115
27Mar97	FG7 ft 4u	Clm50000	6f	22 36	:45 57	1:10 02	93	8/8	3	4 2	4 2	2 hd	2 hd	Ardoin,R	117
17Mar97	FG7 gd 4u	Clm25000	①a1 1/4	:50 22	1:15 08	1:47 38	85	1/12	2 hd	2 hd	3 1	1 1 1/2	2 2	Ardoin,R	119
08Mar97	FG7 ft 4u	Clm25000	6f	21 98	:45 27	1:10 26	90	5/6	4	4 2 1/2	4 2	2 1/4	1 1	Ardoin,R	119
23Feb97	FG8 ft 4u	Clm25000	1 40	:46 70	1:11 48	1:39 86	89	5/8	3 3	3 1	1 hd	1 1/2	2 2	Ardoin,R	119
Workouts:	14Jul LS 3 ft :35.60 h 2/8				07Jul LS 5 ft 1:03.20 b 8/13										

more, he was unable to make up the ground. Note also that in his two attempts to try a longer distance, he had enough speed to get the lead, but failed to hold on.

It does indicate, however, that under certain circumstances such as a class drop or better rating, he may last at a mile. Darla's Charge has a definite running style, and as a handicapper your job is to spot a race where his style is best suited.

When he finds his spot, he is a very dangerous and consistent horse. There are many like this horse. Although he can make the lead in a short race, he prefers not to do so. On an occasion, when asked to try for the lead, he failed to win. Darla's Charge is not a good play if you determine he will be on the lead.

Another obvious running style is the closer. This is the horse that rarely breaks near the lead, and usually makes up ground on the leader in the stretch. The closer is a horse that has the most difficulty changing running styles. A true closer is very uncomfortable using his speed in the early part of a race. He prefers to be unhurried out of the gate, allowed to settle into stride, and at a certain point in the race he begins to run.

When a closer is asked to stay near to the pace he usually gets tired from running too fast too early.

Many fans will not understand why, when a closer got near the early lead, he didn't draw away from the field in the stretch. The reason is that a closer will usually tire if asked to press a pace. It goes against his grain; it is unnatural for him. A true closer may be able to close at any distance. Whether he goes long or short, he must be allowed to settle into stride at his own pace.

A good example of a true closer is the horse Abster the Ghost. You will see that she never runs well unless she is coming from behind, regardless of the distance. (See chart).

Look at the race she ran on March 13. She was closer to the early pace. She was second by two at the second call, then finished third.

Another classic example of a true closer is the horse Never Late Mate. (See chart). You can see that at *no* time in his past performances was he nearer than fifth at the first call, and never did he have the lead at the second call.

Never Late Mate needs to make one late run, and can be very effective when the rider shows the patience to wait until the last part of the race to let him go, as was the case on July 12.

Some horses run in both long and short races and have completely different styles for both. Take the case of Wavering Silk. (See chart).

Red
1
5-2

John L. Pierce II (Navasota, TX)
Orange, White "P", White Sash

Joseph Duhon

Claim Price: **$10,000**

Wavering Silk (TX) **(L)** **122** **Marlon St. Julien**
Ch.f.4 Wavering Monarch-Smooth Like Silk by Damascus (345-61-46-37)
Breeder: Kellie Creek Farm, Inc.,TX (February 25, 1993)

25Jun97	LS9	ft	3uf (S)	Clm10000nw3/L	7f	$:22^{40}$	$:45^{40}$	$1:24^{68}$	**74**	7/13	3	$7^{2\frac{3}{4}}$	$4^{1\frac{1}{2}}$	1^{2}	1^{4}	Lanerie,C	122
07Jun97	LS10	ft	3uf (S)	Clm10000	$1\frac{1}{16}$	$:47^{90}$	$1:13^{36}$	$1:48^{33}$	**62**	2/12	$1^{1\frac{1}{2}}$	1^{1}	$1^{2\frac{1}{2}}$	1^{5}	$1^{5\frac{1}{2}}$	Lanerie,C	122
23May97	LS2	ft	3uf (S)	Clm10000nw2/L	$5\frac{1}{2}$f	$:22^{42}$	$:46^{45}$	$1:05^{87}$	**70**	6/11	9	$8^{3\frac{1}{2}}$	$6^{1\frac{3}{4}}$	3^{5}	$2^{3\frac{3}{4}}$	Lanerie,C	122
10May97	LS2	ft	3uf (S)	Clm9000nw2/L	6f	$:22^{26}$	$:45^{92}$	$1:12^{67}$	**52**	13/13	6	$6^{4\frac{1}{2}}$	5^{5}	$9^{6\frac{1}{2}}$	9^{10}	Lanerie,C	118
26Apr97	LS10	sy	3uf (S)	Clm10000nw2/L	$6\frac{1}{2}$f	$:22^{33}$	$:46^{50}$	$1:20^{77}$	**46**	9/14	5	$7^{5\frac{1}{4}}$	7^{8}	7^{11}	8^{12}	Meche,D	122
17Nov96	Hou3	ft	3uf (S)	Alw7600nw2/L	7f	$:22^{90}$	$:46^{79}$	$1:26^{32}$	**28**	6/7	1	1^{hd}	2^{hd}	$5^{4\frac{1}{4}}$	$7^{30\frac{3}{4}}$	Dupuy,A	118
03Nov96	Hou9	ft	3uf	Clm20000nw2/L	1^{70}	$:47^{73}$	$1:13^{76}$	$1:45^{09}$	**53**	8/11	2^{hd}	1^{hd}	$2^{\frac{1}{2}}$	2^{3}	8^{12}	Lanerie,C	114
06Oct96	Hou8	ft	3uf (S)	Alw8000nw1/x	1^{70}	$:47^{92}$	$1:13^{83}$	$1:45^{87}$	**65**	3/5	2^{hd}	2^{1}	3^{nk}	1^{hd}	2^{nk}	Dupuy,A	119
21Sep96	Ret7	ft	3uf (S)	MisionTrai-25k	6f	$:21^{98}$	$:44^{92}$	$1:10^{24}$	**62**	9/11	10	$10^{7\frac{1}{2}}$	$10^{10\frac{1}{4}}$	11^{14}	$10^{14\frac{1}{4}}$	Dupuy,A	117
12Sep96	Ret8	ft	34f	Alw8200nw2/L	6f	$:22^{38}$	$:45^{84}$	$1:11^{30}$	**62**	2/7	5	5^{3}	$4^{2\frac{1}{2}}$	3^{4}	3^{5}	Stanton,T	118

Workouts: 21Jun LS 3 ft :37.00 b 7/17 17Apr LS 6 ft 1:12.80 h 3/8

Wavering Silk's running styles are different, but predictable. When she is entered in a long race, she tries for the lead. She has the speed to be close, or on top, but does not have a closing kick necessary to come from off the pace in a route race. When sprinting, she does not have the speed to keep up in the early going. However, Wavering Silk possesses sufficient stamina to close ground. Although she does not reach the winner's circle all that often, you can certainly tell where she will be in a particular race, depending on the distance. She won the outing of June 7 going one-mile and one-sixteenth wire to wire, then came from behind to win June 25 at seven furlongs.

One of the biggest errors made by handicappers is to determine that a particular horse will make it to the front of a field. Some horses rarely go to the lead, but when finding a soft field void of early speed, they are capable of going to the front and winning with ease. Look at Nicole C. (See chart). Only once was she able to go to the lead, in a race lacking speed.

Red
1
5-2

Five Star Racing, Ltd. (Garland, TX)
White, Red and Blue Blocks, Red Star on White Ball, White Stripe on Blue Sleeves

Jim Gaston

Nicole C. **(L)** **116** **Ronald Ardoin**
Ch.m.5 Superbity-Feels Like Love by Northern Jove (390-80-62-48)
Breeder: Chris Drakos,KY (March 2, 1992)

04Jul97	LS2	ft	3uf	Clm7500	6f	$:22^{35}$	$:45^{50}$	$1:11^{05}$	**61**	7/9	8	$7^{7\frac{3}{4}}$	$7^{8\frac{3}{4}}$	5^{11}	$6^{17\frac{1}{2}}$	Ardoin,R	114
21Jun97	LS10	ft	3uf	Clm6250	6f	$:21^{87}$	$:45^{80}$	$1:12^{26}$	**74**	5/9	6	3^{4}	$4^{1\frac{1}{2}}$	3^{1}	$2^{\frac{1}{2}}$	Cloninger,W	119
13Jun97	LS9	ft	3uf	Clm6250	1	$:46^{59}$	$1:12^{82}$	$1:40^{09}$	**68**	2/11	4^{9}	$3^{6\frac{1}{2}}$	$3^{\frac{1}{2}}$	1^{hd}	$2^{1\frac{1}{2}}$	Cloninger,W	116
07Jun97	LS1	ft	3uf	Clm6250	$6\frac{1}{2}$f	$:22^{35}$	$:45^{75}$	$1:18^{40}$	**68**	8/11	9	$8^{5\frac{1}{4}}$	5^{4}	$2^{2\frac{1}{2}}$	3^{4}	Cloninger,W	119
25May97	LS2	ft	3uf	Clm5000nw/y	6f	$:22^{17}$	$:45^{28}$	$1:12^{12}$	**73**	2/9	8	9^{8}	$4^{7\frac{1}{2}}$	3^{4}	$3^{2\frac{3}{4}}$	Cloninger,W	119
25Apr97	LS3	sy	3uf	Clm6250	6f	$:22^{76}$	$:45^{85}$	$1:11^{80}$	**79**	1/6	1	1^{hd}	$1^{1\frac{1}{2}}$	$1^{3\frac{1}{2}}$	$1^{3\frac{3}{4}}$	Cloninger,W	116
26Sep96	Lad4	ft	3uf	Clm4000	6f	$:22^{98}$	$:46^{71}$	$1:12^{97}$	**66**	5/10	8	$8^{5\frac{3}{4}}$	$6^{5\frac{1}{2}}$	6^{9}	$5^{6\frac{3}{4}}$	Cloninger,W	119
12Sep96	Lad4	ft	3uf	Clm5000nw2/3m	6f	$:22^{61}$	$:45^{97}$	$1:11^{82}$	**67**	9/11	10	$11^{11\frac{3}{4}}$	$8^{9\frac{1}{2}}$	$6^{4\frac{1}{2}}$	$4^{5\frac{1}{2}}$	Gonzalez,C	116
21Aug96	Lad1	ft	3uf	Clm4000	6f	$:22^{77}$	$:45^{98}$	$1:12^{14}$	**74**	5/8	2	5^{6}	5^{4}	$4^{2\frac{3}{4}}$	1^{nk}	Cloninger,W	116

Nicole C. hadn't had the lead before her April 25 win and didn't get it again in subsequent races.

The running style of each horse in each race should be determined to see what type of horse benefits most from the way the race will be run. Almost as important as class and condition is *how the race shapes up.*

A classy horse which is in condition, and draws an outside post in a race where three or four horses inside of him also have the speed to break with him may *never* be able to overcome his position. The best play anyone can make is when finding a single speed horse in a race. If he has class enough and is in form, he should be an easy winner. This type of horse can win a greater percentage of the time than almost any other.

When handicapping a race in which all horses have early speed, look for a closer to benefit from the dueling on the lead. Remember one thing— that if the race shapes up for a front runner or a closer, the horse you choose *must* have the ability and the fitness to win. Just choosing a closer in a field where there is early speed is not enough. Even under the best of conditions a horse rarely wins when over his head or in poor physical condition.

A good handicapper will study very carefully the running style of each horse entered. From this he determines what type of horse is best suited to win and: *he runs the race over in his mind before the race is actually run.*

You should be able to see exactly where you believe each horse in the race will be at each call. Naturally, this won't work precisely, but you get the proper *mental* picture of which horse fits the race regarding running style.

If you can picture three horses battling for the lead, and there is a fit horse with class enough who draws a favorable post position *and* who races his best when just off the pace—you may have an excellent play. It is very important to study all the lines in the horse's past performances so that you have a true picture of his running style. Don't be swayed by one race or even two.

Where a horse finished in his previous race may—or may not—be of consequence. It does show the horse's willingness to finish ahead of other horses. If nothing else, it indicates his *ability* to finish ahead of the other horses.

This isn't truly indicative of what he will do in the present race, as many last-place finishers have come back to win the next time out. Where a horse finishes in his past few races should not affect your handicapping of where he will finish on this occasion. A horse may have been way back in his latest few, but is very capable of winning in his next.

One certain thing is that horses which finish far back have not expended much energy in doing so. Often when horses have been badly beaten, the jockey lets up on them causing them to finish farther back than they ordinarily would. If a horse is not going to be in the money, or get a check for his owner, it makes no difference how far back he is.

Whether a horse is consistent certainly matters. I would prefer to play a horse that runs close at the finish in nearly all of his races. Unfortunately, horses that are close up at the finish frequently go off at low odds. If you can ignore the fact that a horse finished last the time before, you may get a nice return when he wins next time.

A final thing to remember is that horses are capable of changing running styles. Many times a horse has been asked to run to the lead by his trainer when he would be better suited to close. Trainers are constantly changing techniques with horses trying to find the secret that makes them run better. Most of the time, even when attempting to change a horse's running style, the trainer is unable to do so. The horse, through conformation and temperament, is only able to run a certain way. When you see a horse run an improved race after changing style, you may look to see the next style next time out.

Pay some attention also to a horse that changed his style the time before, but had no success. A front runner that is not asked for speed in a particular race, but makes up some ground at the end, may go back to his true style next time, and have added endurance. If he had the ability to make up ground the time before, he should be able to hang on longer next time he gets the lead.

Now and then a closer is asked to *press* the pace in a race. The trainer may be trying to get some speed out of the horse for subsequent races. Although the closer falters when trying for the lead, the race is a good tightener for his next start where he returns to his running style. An unsuccessful change in running style often is a prep for a horse to come back with his true style and be much improved.

CHAPTER 16

Jockeys!

Many argue about the role of the jockey in horse racing. A jockey's role varies in importance given by different handicappers. Some have said that the jockey counts for less than ten percent in the horse's ability to win; other say it is of prime importance.

I believe without question that the jockey has a major role in determining horse races. In many instances he spells the difference between victory and defeat. I have gone so far as to eliminate certain jockeys whenever they ride, regardless of the horses they are on. I have found some to be so incompetent that I refuse to wager even one cent on them at any time.

My theory is based on observation and facts. Let me begin by saying that it's a foolish notion that all jockeys are fairly equal, and that the horse does the running—or that the best horse will win with any jockey.

This is hogwash.

In no profession in the world is everyone nearly equal. There are bad shoe salesmen and there are good shoe salesmen, bad doctors and good doctors, bad lawyers and good ones. So with jockeys. It is inconceivable to me how people can believe that in a profession as skilled as race riding everyone is much the same.

A jockey needs many skills. He must be intelligent so that he can size up races and react instantaneously to conditions. He must have the ability to think quickly and clearly, plus excellent reflexes and be able to adapt. A jockey also needs strength sufficient to hold and guide a one-thousand-pound animal.

He must have compassion for the horse, and understanding of the personality of each one that he rides. He needs an ability to communicate with the horse. He must be a hard worker, in excellent physical condition and be able to learn from his mistakes.

A jockey is a true athlete who needs combined skills necessary to make him a success.

To say that all jockeys are nearly equal is like saying all baseball players are equal, all quarterbacks pass the same way, and all tennis players have generally the same ability.

The scale difference between good and bad jockeys would be the same as in any other profession. Some are very good and some very bad, with many merely average. When a race is determined by inches, fifths of second and sometimes eyelashes—it is ridiculous to believe that the good rider wouldn't make the difference.

After examining all the necessary tools and attributes of a good jockey, there is one intangible factor that I find difficult to describe—but I know it is there just as sure as I'm alive.

That is the way a jockey *sits and moves on a horse.* I have not been a rider. I do not know the techniques of riding. I can only use my senses in spotting the difference. Some jockeys have the ability to sit quietly still and ride smoothly to make the horse run faster and with more fluidity than before.

I have seen many riders who actually seem to work against the horse; these cause him to have poor action and slow him down considerably.

It would seem foolish to assume that Bill Shoemaker won so many races because he always got the better horse. Steve Cauthen must have had something more than the best mounts. This is true of any of the top riders.

I always feel that the poor riders—the losers—will find a way to lose. They will either break badly, race wide, get trapped or whatever other way they can find to lose. They lack confidence; they make the crucial mistake at the wrong time and get beaten. All jockeys win *some* races. When the conditions are right and everything goes well, the poorest of them will get home first. Horse players must work with percentages, however, and it seems a bad risk to play a jockey who wins less than ten percent of the time.

I don't believe that the reason certain riders lead the standings year in and year out is because they get the best horses. Because they are better, they eventually receive the better mounts. But they all start the same; the better ones go on.

Statistics reveal that a small percentage of riders win the majority of races. If one were to keep figures at a certain meeting, he would find that the top ten riders will win 60 to 75 percent of their races, while the rest of the races are divided among the majority.

It must also be remembered that jockeys who ride less frequently have their skill dulled by inactivity. If you ride one horse a day, it is difficult to stay sharp and fit. It would be similar to a baseball player coming to bat only fifty times in a season. You certainly couldn't expect him to be at his best. When backing a seldom-used rider, you are taking that chance. Would you call for a pinch hitter in the ninth inning of a crucial baseball game when he has been to bat just a few times all year?

Jockeys who ride sparingly are also under much more pressure than the top riders. They know that the only way to get more mounts is to win. When they get just a few mounts they must make the most of each ride. This naturally causes such a jockey to be under pressure. Mistakes are made under pressure. Jockeys who are under pressure are less apt to wait on a horse and they have less patience. They move prematurely and use up a horse's energies too fast. They lose ground when a little patience would have found the rail opening up.

All of this adds up to an important factor. *The jockey who rides the horse you select should be a competent one.* The majority of riders at most tracks are **capable** of winning. But some win so rarely that you must never play them; instead, go with the percentages.

If attending a meeting on a regular basis, I advise you to keep records of jockeys. You should know when a rider has one win in one hundred mounts. You should also make mental notes of which jockeys seem to be better on front runners, which on closers, etc. When finalizing a selection, be sure you are not compromising your chances by playing a poor rider or one who does not fit the horse. You should develop a good working knowledge of all riders on the grounds and use this knowledge in making final decisions.

The jockey plays a major role in which horse wins and loses at racetracks. Do not make the mistake of believing the riders are not important. To be a thorough handicapper you must be aware of all the variables that go into picking a winner; *the jockey cannot be overlooked.*

In many races, the jockey will not be an important factor in making your final decision on a horse. However, in many other races it can be the difference between your winning and losing. Get to know the riders and be selective; it pays off.

You should know another thing about jockeys. Many times a jockey could have ridden two or more horses in a particular race in their last appearance. Many handicappers feel that the choice of the jockey is unquestionably the better horse.

It should be understood how the choices are made. First of all, a jockey rarely has anything to say regarding what he rides. Nearly all jockeys have agents; these secure the mounts for the riders.

The jockeys seldom know which horses they will ride on a given day; they learn this from the *Racing Form* or program for the day's races. Sometimes they first learn the horse's name when they mount the horse in the paddock.

The agent is solely responsible for the jockey's mounts and where there is a choice to be made, the agent makes it.

To believe that the rider who has ridden two or more horses in a race will choose the best one to ride that day is erroneous. The *agent* will handicap the race—just as you do—and try to pick the right one. All they have in their favor is that they need not try to decide from among the entire field—just two or three horses. The agent may be right *most* of the time, but his decision should not be regarded as definitely the right one.

On occasion, neither the jockey nor agent has his choice. The agent may have committed his rider to a trainer for a horse's next race long before he knew what the competition would be. When an agent gives first call to a trainer, he rarely gets out of the agreement.

One final reason for the jockey being on a particular horse is that he may ride almost exclusively for one trainer. Whenever the trainer has a horse entered in a race, that jockey must ride him.

Speaking of jockey changes, I always consider it a plus when a horse goes form an obscure or untalented rider to one of the better jockeys. The rider switch may be all that a horse needs to improve enough to win. I would *not* play a poor horse just because he obtains the services of a top rider. If the horse has shown some run with inferior riders, then suddenly gets a top jockey, he may be worth a play.

Conversely, if a horse goes from a top rider to one of lesser ability, I believe this to be a negative factor. If the horse was unable to win with a good jockey, he could probably not win with the lesser rider. A change from one good jockey to another capable rider, which happens often, should not be regarded as important.

A last point concerning jockeys: Many riders are more adept at a certain style than others. For instance, a jockey may be very good at getting a horse out of the gate and an excellent sprint rider. Another may be better when having the opportunity to rate a horse over a distance of ground. When you can solidly identify a certain jockey having a certain style, you may employ this fact into your handicapping.

If, for example, you were playing a sprint and you felt that a certain horse would be an excellent play *if* he could break on top, and the jockey riding that horse is known to be a good gate boy (breaks well from the gate), this would enhance his chances and may be the major factor in determining your play.

You should have some knowledge regarding this point, and although the majority of riders can ride at any distance equally well, some are much better on a particular horse and it should be recognized.

CHAPTER 17

Post position

When handicapping a horse race, after answering the questions of class and fitness, one must learn to separate the contenders. One of the most important of all variables is that of post position, a factor that can make the best horse a loser and a long shot a winner.

Some people maintain that post position is of little importance to the outcome of a race. This statement pays small regard to mathematics, which is a much more exacting science than handicapping. Mathematics tells you that the total distance of a larger circumference is greater than the distance of a smaller one. A race track is oval in shape. The circumference of the inner rail is much shorter than that of the outer rail. This basically explains that horses that save ground by running closer to the inside will run a shorter distance during a race than those running farther removed from the inner rail. This mathematical fact is impossible to refute.

When jockeys are being interviewed, they invariably speak of the shortest way home—getting to the rail. There are times, naturally, when a horse runs wider than others at certain points in the race and still wins. The rail becomes clogged at times and the rider must swing outside to gain running room. There are many reasons for running to the outside at some point in the race. The important thing to know is: *How far must the horse remain wide?* If a horse is forced to stay wide throughout the running of an entire race, he runs a greater distance and would have to be far superior to win.

In calculating which horse will lose the most ground, there are some important principles to understand. I will take this time to go over those principles and explain their application.

Let's first look at *sprinting*. The majority of tracks race from five to seven furlongs with a start on the backstretch. Many sprints are started from a chute which is a straightaway extending from the backstretch. This allows the horses to run in a straight line for a longer period of time, which cuts down the burden placed on outside horses. The shorter the run to the first turn, the more difficult it is for the outside horses. Horses do not lose ground until they reach the turns. It is on the turns—when forced wide—that the most ground is lost. In five- and five-and-one-half-furlong races, the run to the turn is generally very short.

When handicapping the outside horses, you must feel that they have the early speed to race into quick contention and be no more than three wide. This means that you must determine who has the speed inside, and how many will reach the turn on even terms.

In your calculations remember that in order for the outside horses to get the rail, they must be *at least a length and a half faster to the turn than the inside horses* or else they will not be able to move to the inside without fouling.

Actually, three wide is still difficult to overcome, but the best horse in the race by a few lengths can overcome running three wide and still win. If I see that a horse will be four wide, or more, I discount his chances. Now and then, unforeseen things happen and the outside horse will gain better position than expected down the backside and to the turn. But we must deal in percentages and for the most part, your diagnosis will be correct and the outside horse will lose too much ground.

If a horse in question is an even-running horse, such as Darla's Charge (illustrated in a previous chapter), the outside post position usually spells death to a bettor's chances. A horse that desires to lay about third or fourth, then closes on the leaders, will lose more ground than he can stand to lose. He does not have the speed to get the lead, nor does he have the closing ability to drop far off the pace. His only hope is to break as close as he can, then hope a gap opens up down the backside where he can drop over. This can also be determined by the running styles of the other horses.

An example would be when there are a few early-speed horses in a race and the rest are slow beginners. You may anticipate that the even-running horse may find a place to drop over. On other occasions, you can easily determine that the even-running horse will be fanned out nearly the entire trip, which will doom his chances. In general, the even-running horse who tries to stay just behind the early leaders is the poorest play when drawing a post position on or near the outside.

The late-running horse, or fast closer, may not be hurt as much as the even-running one, but is still in a lot of trouble. He obviously does not have the speed to keep up in the early going, so the jockey's only hope is to drop him back to last or near the end, try to save some ground by letting the rest of the field go, then attempt to make one late run.

This position is very precarious in short races such as five- and five-and-one-half furlongs. By the time he gets his position, he is usually so far behind that he can hardly see the leaders. He then must wade through traffic and hope that the leaders or those just behind have no stamina. In a short race, you must assume that some of the horses can run that distance without tiring. A closer trying to make up ground on a horse that is not tiring is in trouble.

A major reason why outside horses have difficulties is that they are used up more than others trying to get into contention in the early part of the race. A horse with speed must be forced to break with urgency in order to outbreak the inside horses. If the horse is a known quitter, his speed is used up in trying to get position and he has nothing left for the drive.

A speed horse must be able to get near the lead without expending an unusual amount of energy and without being forced wide on the turns in order to have a decent chance to win. An even-running horse is also sent out much faster than he would like in the early running to seek a favorable position. I have seen many of the even-running types rush from the gate so as to avoid being forced outside the entire field. When this horse is set down for the stretch run, he often has little stamina left. Even the closers are asked to break more alertly in hopes of getting the rail somewhere down the backside and are used up much too early.

In sprints of short distances, the inside post positions have a distinct advantage, barring track biases. I must make this exception because some tracks have a definite track bias for the outside and away from the rail. At the now defunct Lincoln Downs in Rhode Island, I found the horses in the number one position in five-furlong races winning infrequently. Hollywood Park is also noted for death and the rail being synonymous. When a track bias is of this nature, you must understand it and make the proper adjustments.

When the rail is bad, those horses in post positions two, three, and four, etc. are not hampered as much. Usually it is the number one hole that is the trouble spot. When no bias is evident, however, the inside horses save the ground. A speed horse can be sent into contention without undue urging. The jockey can settle him into position by edging up on the rail without being used. When he hits the turn, he will naturally be able to save the ground.

Even-runners and closers benefit from running nearer the inside. An even-runner can move along with the pack without losing ground and expending too much energy—then, with racing luck, can find himself in strong contention when the serious running begins.

A late runner also has an advantage because he does not have to maneuver for position. He can be allowed to settle into stride without losing ground and run when asked.

There is one danger to the inside at *all* times, and that is the possibility of being blocked. Closers have the most difficulty because they usually get behind most of the field and may find it jammed up when making their big runs. Closers are better spotted somewhere in the middle of the pack. A closer may benefit greatly , though when the rail opens up by the lead horses drifting out. Should this happen, the late runner has an easy time of it. Horses with speed do *not* encounter as much traffic and usually benefit the most from saving ground.

In races from six- to seven-and-a-half furlongs, the outside posts have a slightly better chance. The farther the run down the backside, the more chance the outside horses have to find a spot to tuck in. When your handicapping tells you that a horse will run outside all the way down the backside and into the turn, the horse should be eliminated. Speed horses and closers may not be as much affected by post position over six furlongs, but the even-runners are always at a disadvantage from the outside.

Remember that running style and post position go hand in hand. You must determine the running style of every horse, decide where it will be at certain points, especially at the break and on the turns, then decide if the post position is good for its style.

Even in long races of a mile or more, inside post positions have an advantage. In races of one mile, the run to the first turn is very short on most tracks. Outside horses must either gun to the turn to try to make it on top, or be held back to avoid being fanned extremely wide.

Closers are not often affected by post position in races at a mile or over because they can drop back and still have plenty of time to rally. Horses that need to be close or in the lead will be hurt by drawing the outside. I must clarify one thing. When I speak of the "outside," I don't necessarily mean the *extreme* outside post position. In a seven-horse field, the sixth horse is outside when all five inside horses will break with him. Your determination usually is: How far outside will my horse have to run and for how long?

As the distance of the race lengthens, the post position becomes less of a factor. However, I don't care for horses with early or even-running speed which draw the far outside at *any* distance unless I feel the animals can get the lead easily enough. In a long race, you certainly don't want to see your horse running at top speed out of the gate so as to get position. When he has to run a mile-and-a-sixteenth, it's better to be reserved as much as possible in the early going.

Post position can be so important that it can make a ten-length winner of his last race come back against the same field and finish last on the next try.

Consider, for example, a twelve-horse field. A speed horse drew the two hole last time, was allowed to break in stride, ease up along the rail into contention, save ground on the turn while the rest were being forced wide, hit the stretch with speed in reserve, and drew out as much the best.

The next week he draws the twelve post with much the same field. He is forced out of the gate, asked to run with urgency to reach contention, but finds himself four wide with the leaders on the turn. Losing ground with every step, he drops back and finishes dead last. It happens all the time.

A common way to spot longshots is by looking carefully over their post positions in previous races. At times, you will find a fit horse has had no chance to win because of a bad post in each of his last three, four, or more races. When drawing an inside or a more favorable post, he becomes a winner. If a horse has been badly placed a number of times, and has finished up the track, the fans ordinarily send him off at long odds. *This is your chance to select a horse at long odds with an excellent chance of winning.*

Barring track bias or idiosyncrasies which necessitate a horse running wide, it is advantageous to stay close to the rail during a race. Horses that stay closest to the rail for the longest periods of time during a race end up running a much shorter distance. When races are won by such scant margins, it is the rare horse that can run many yards farther than his opponents and still win—although it does happen. A horse that runs on the rail throughout, then swings wide in the drive, loses little ground. But the one which is fanned wide for a good portion of the race is in trouble.

In your handicapping, determine the running style of each horse. Then determine which ones, due to their style, will be forced to lose more ground than they can afford. Few horses can afford to lose ground. Favor speed horses on the inside, be sure they can make the lead with relative ease when on the outside. Closers are better placed in the middle of the pack, but have a disadvantage in very short races when on the outside. Closers are not affected by post position in long races.

The careful study and proper use and interpretations of post position can select more long shots for you than any other single factor, and can eliminate more losing favorites than any other factor. It is certainly pleasant to be able to throw out the favorite and be confident he won't win because of a bad post position. This is where you can make your money. You still must answer the question of fitness and class, but post position further narrows down the field and helps you select the horse with enough class, one that is fit, and is in a favorable position to take advantage of its running style and run to his maximum potential.

CHAPTER 18

Speed rating and track variant

D*aily Racing Form* breaks down the running times of horses in races by a formula which gives you a numerical indication of how fast they ran. The speed rating is derived from the track record for that distance. The base number of speed rating is 100. If the track record for six furlongs at a particular track is 1:08, the running time in subsequent races of 1:08 gets a speed rating of 100. For every one-fifth of a second removed from 1:08, the horse will lose one point (or gain one point, if he beats it) on his rating.

An example of this follows: A horse runs in a six-furlong race at a track where the track record for that distance is 1:08. The race is run in 1:10. He finishes behind the leader by two lengths. Removing one point for each fifth of a second away from the track record, you will see that the horse loses 10 points because he was two seconds from the record. Two seconds breaks down to ten fifths. This gives the horse a rating of 90 after subtracting the ten points from the base of 100. If he breaks the record, his rating would be over 100.

This is a simplified way of telling you the time the horse had in his previous race in comparison with other horses in the race without having to use your own mathematics. The speed rating only refers to finishing time and has nothing to do with fractional time.

The track variant is a number shown in *Daily Racing Form* just to the right of the speed rating. The number is derived from averaging the times of the races at a track on a certain day. The higher the number, the slower the track may have been. Averaging the times on a particular day may indicate that either the track was slower or faster, or that the caliber of horses was better or poorer. On weekends, when racetracks present their better programs with better horses, the average time of the races is faster, showing a lower track variant. When the track is "off," meaning muddy, sloppy, etc., the track variant is usually much higher. The variant may also indicate when a track which is listed as fast was actually faster on a given day.

I have spent these paragraphs explaining speed rating and track variant so that you will know what you are using when applying these numbers to your handicapping. How to use and interpret the numbers if of prime importance and I will now explain it.

During the past few years I have paid less and still less attention to speed ratings, almost to the point of ignoring them completely. The speed rating is simply an indication of final running time, a variable I find to be of little or no use in most cases.

If you will refer to the previous chapter on the use of final times in handicapping, you will see that I feel this to be one of the lesser tools to be used in handicapping. Consequently, I am in little need of another number that points out running time.

The speed rating can only be used when comparing horses that have run the same distance at the same track under the same conditions. You cannot compare a speed rating of a horse who ran at six-and-a-half furlongs in his last, with one who raced at six furlongs. The track record from which the speed rating is based may be very different. For example, a horse who shipped in from a major track to a minor track, under ideal conditions, may have set an exceptionally fast track record for six-and-a-half furlongs. This means that in subsequent races the speed ratings will always be relatively low. This would make it impossible to compare speed ratings at different distances. To do so would be like comparing eggs with baseballs.

Horses that acquired a speed rating at another track for the same distance would, for the same reason, not be comparable with speed ratings from the new track. To expect validity from speed ratings, one would hope to find a race where most of the horses had competed at the same distance at the same track; then you could at least tell who ran the fastest.

But, then you would have to apply the track variant to your calculations to be sure that the times were achieved under similar circumstances.

The question always becomes: Is a speed rating of 80 with a track variant of 16 better than a speed rating of 76 with a track variant of 20?

Some racetracks have such varying degrees of track surfaces during a meeting—especially Eastern tracks in the winter—that trying to apply a logical formula to speed ratings and track variants is nearly impossible.

The major question remains: Is running time of any value in handicapping?

I have found over my years as a handicapper that running time, unless extremely better than others, is of little importance. I have found cheap horses running faster times than expensive horses; then, when they meet, the cheap horses finish behind. There are so many reasons why the final time is what it is, that it would be impossible to make any workable formula. The reason is that the average racegoer has very few facts on hand as to why the times of races were what they were.

I have seen many handicappers take the speed rating and track variant, add up the two numbers, and feel that the horse with the highest number will be the winner. Anyone over the age of seven can add up two numbers. If this were all there was to handicapping, every horse in every race would pay $2.10 and the tracks would be forced out of business. Handicapping is far more than adding up numbers. It is far more than knowing how fast a horse ran in his last race as compared to the other horses in the race. But these times and numbers do have *some* value at certain times.

You may use speed rating and finishing times with more confidence when handicapping 2-year-olds running short distances. These young horses have not established much form, early in the season especially, and may run approximately the same time each time out. They are also free from major infirmities and *can* run the same time each time out.

The use of running times would be of more value in very short races of two or three or four furlongs. The shorter the distance, the less discrepancy there will be in running times, making a fifth of a second more important.

Once 2-year-olds have run a few times and have established some form, running time will be less important. For the most part, the average handicapper spends most of his time handicapping races involving older horses at longer distances. The principles of good handicapping should be mastered for the *important* races. If one were to make his living at handicapping 2-year-olds, he may spend more time with speed ratings.

That brings us to Beyer figures and other services that provide a number for each race. Again, these numbers are primarily a product of final times. Services have also created par times, which tell you the average times horses ran at different tracks and distances for different levels. This is geared to compare a running time from track to track to deal with ship-ins. Once again, if I don't accept the validity of final times in making selections, I can't consider par times either, although I can see where it could be helpful on some occasions.

Once again, every variable has its place, and there may be a few times when a speed rating, a finishing time or a Beyer can be of value to you and spot a good winner. But be aware of speed ratings, Beyers and running times when you are having a hard time separating contenders. Something you see in his Beyer ratings may tell you enough to give him the added edge and give you that extra winner.

In general, however, I pay little attention to speed ratings or track variants. I am much more concerned with answering the questions of fitness and class, but will make use of speed ratings on occasion, always in conjunction with the two basics.

CHAPTER 19

Class and company line

A lthough the factor of class has been discussed in detail in a previous chapter, it is necessary to elaborate further on the subject
because of its high importance in handicapping. The variable of
class is heavily used by nearly all handicappers. However, it is misunder-
stood by many. Class can simply be defined as the company one horse
keeps, or which horses he or she races against.

The handicapper needs to establish which horse has sufficient class in
a race to be determined a strong contender. In many races—especially low-
grade claimers—all horses may be of primarily the same class. If this is the
case, you need to make use of all the other variables in order to separate
the field. In many instances, however, there may be one or more horses
that have a definite class edge. The classier animal, when in condition, has
a definite edge over the field. Percentage-wise, this will give you more
winners than any other single factor. The trick is not just knowing this fact,
but to define the class horses in a race. *This is probably the most difficult
handicapping variable to recognize, and those who are able to master this
variable will become the big winners.*

The class line lists the type of race the horse has been running in
during his most recent races. When in claiming races, the claiming price
will indicate, for the most part, the caliber of horses one horse has campaigned against. Many so-called sophisticated handicappers pay less attention to this claiming price as they gain experience. This is a big mistake.
The claiming price is an excellent indicator of what caliber of horses one
horse has faced.

A group of horses running for a $10,000 claiming tag will be a stronger
group overall than the $5,000 group. At cheaper racetracks, even a small
drop from $5,000 to $4,000 may be significant enough to make a difference. It should not be overlooked.

I would say that the higher the claiming price, the better the overall caliber of horses running in that race. But there are exceptions, and this is what the handicapper must learn.

As outlined in Chapter 3, any race that restricts the entries because of the conditions of the race must be considered weaker than a non-restricted race. The most common restrictions are of age, sex, where bred, number of times won, or since last win, or money won. A $10,000 race for 3-year-olds and up, non-winners of 2, as you can see, is restricted to a certain minority of horses on the grounds. Such a race is bound to attract a weaker field. A $10,000 race for fillies and mares should be considered weaker than its counterpart, open to both sexes.

Any race that restricts the entrants at a particular level is generally weaker than a race open to all comers, and one will notice the use of the word generally, as there are no absolutes in horse racing.

At one time, the *Daily Racing Form* did not include the publishing of conditions, but now, conditions of every race are clearly spelled out so the handicapper can determine the quality of a race at a particular level.

In allowance races, the lowest level is a non-winner of two races, followed by a non-winner of an allowance race, signified by "nw1x" in the past performances. The next level is 2x, then 3x and 4x. The better allowance races restrict the field by money won since a certain time. The non-conditioned races (NC), are the top of the line.

Naturally, a race for non-winners of two lifetime has to be a weak field; no horse in the race has ever won more than once, making this race just one cut above a maiden race.

Other restrictions may be: non-winners of three races lifetime, or four races lifetime. The conditions may restrict races to non-winners during a calendar year and, sometimes, two calendar years. A race for non-winners in 1997-98 can't have much of a field.

Then the conditions may state that a race is for non-winners for a few months. As the restrictions become fewer, more horses are eligible to run in that race, and usually the winners and better horses in that claiming or allowance category are found as the restrictions dwindle.

Handicap competition makes up a very small percentage of the average horse-player's wagers. There are only one or two handicaps per week at most tracks, and none at others. The handicap division is usually so exclusive that the fan usually knows the differences. It must be remembered that a handicap is, in general, more difficult than an allowance race.

There are exceptions to the rule, but these are few. One exception may be when a handicap star decides to drop in to an allowance race as a prep. He may make shambles of the field, leading one to believe the losers were of poor quality. Such may not have been the case.

Another category is the starter allowance or starter handicap races. These races are almost always tougher than a claiming race at a similar price. A $3,500 starter allowance is more difficult than a $3,500 claiming race, and may be as difficult as a $6,500 claimer. Take time to inspect each horse to see at what claiming level it raced previously before entering the starter series. This may give you a good indication as to what he can handle. Remember, however, that *any* horse that comes from either starter series into a claiming spot is dropping in class, provided the claiming race is similar to the starter price.

In starters, the horses are not eligible to be claimed. This is a fine spot for a hard-hitting horse that runs out of conditions. He can remain in competition without fear of being claimed and without undue penalties.. The starters always attract the better horses running in the lower claiming ranks.

In maiden races, one should follow the same formula. If it is a claiming race, it is usually inferior to an allowance race for maidens. The only exception is when the claiming price is up around $50,000, where the trainer feels there is little chance of being claimed.

Among lower-priced maidens, the same horses will usually run within $5,000 or $10,000 of their established worth. A $5,000 maiden race may find the same horses in it that ran in a $10,000 maiden race a week ago. The company line, which I will explain shortly, will tell you a lot about this.

In again touching upon 2-year-old races, I firmly feel that 2-year-old maiden races with a number of first-time starters are as unpredictable as New England weather. Of all the races to ignore on a card, this type leads the list. When the juveniles become winners, or have run enough races to have established some form, they can become highly predictable. Use the same handicapping principles used in selecting any other race for the babies and you should have a high percentage of winners.

Company line

Gong hand-in-hand with class is the *company line*—the place near the end of the past performance line where *Daily Racing Form* lists the first three finishers in past races. This line can be the most revealing of all when determining class. It is of little importance when visiting a track where you don't know one horse from the other. It is of great importance when following a meeting or circuit and when you can recognize the horses by name.

The company line tells you *the level of competition being kept by the horse*. This still remains the key to selecting winners. Who did the horse race against? What could be more important? If I were handicapping a horse that had run fourth in his previous race, I would want to know which horses were first, second, and third. If, in my opinion, any of the first three finishers *could* have won the race coming up, then the fourth-place finisher in that race would look good in this spot. As a regular, you would know by name the better horses running at a track, the speed horses, the closers, etc.

If I were handicapping a race where a front runner was badly beaten last time, I would be interested in knowing by whom. If the winner were a strong front runner with top early speed, I might feel that this horse in question had no chance in that race against a horse that was able to run him off his feet in the early going. How far back he finished may be of little consequence. In fact, the farther back the better in most cases.

The company line also points out horses which were beaten by another than may have dropped drastically in company. If you know that a $5,000 race was actually won by a horse dropping down from $7,500, you can give the horses in closest contention a solid excuse for not winning. Knowing whom they ran against can give you a large edge over the players who go to the races on occasions and are not familiar with the stock.

One of the major determinations I always make is: How do I feel the first three finishers in a horse's previous race would do in *this* race?

At times I can spot when all three of them could win the upcoming race. This makes a great case for a horse coming from the race; usually the price is right.

There is one point I would like to clarify concerning class. Many racetracks now card graduated claiming races. That is, any horse may be entered anywhere from $12,000 to $16,000 in a particular race. The cheaper the horse runs for, the greater weight allowance he receives. These races can become confusing when trying to decide on class. You may make mistake a horse that ran for $12,000 as being cheaper than one who ran for

$16,000. Such a horse may, in fact, have run against the exact same company. One must go to the conditions again to make a distinction.

Discovering the true class of a horse is not an easy task. *When the technique is mastered, however, the handicapper will find his profits will increase dramatically.* Be very painstaking in making your class judgement. And be certain that your selection has the *class* to win.

You must remember one thing more about class. Many horses move up in class and win. The percentage is not in your favor, but still, many do. A horse that wins for $5,000 by five lengths may well be able to handle $7,500 horses next time.

One of the most difficult determinations to make is whether recent winners can handle class jumps. When uncertain, you have an unplayable race, at least not with serious money. Younger horses may be able to improve with each race and climb the ladder.

Older horses that have established their class over the years most often do *not* climb beyond what you would expect. They may get good and win over their assumed heads for a race or two, but soon find their Waterloos and come back to earth.

Younger horses (three, four or five) may climb from the claiming ranks to the handicap division without stopping. You are still dealing with percentages, though, and in general horses have a level of competition at which they can successfully compete and will be outrun when over their heads. You may miss a horse moving up that wins, but you will more than make up for it when you have many class horses winning while the lesser ones fall by the wayside at short odds after easy wins against weaker competition.

How many horses in the race?

I will include in this chapter the final number shown at the very end of the past performance line. This is the number of horses which competed in the race.

The statistic may have special significance in many races and should not be treated lightly.

It is always more difficult to win a $5,000 race with twelve horses in it than it is to win a $5,000 race with six horses. The more horses in a race, the more you have to beat, and the more trouble you can get into. One of the major reasons why a given best horse does not win is because of bad racing luck. In a bulky field, all kinds of things can happen.

When I handicap a race, I always take note of how many horses were beaten by the horse I'm handicapping. If he ran third in a five-horse field, it means he beat only two horses. This is hardly enough to get excited about.

A horse that ran fifth in a twelve-horse field probably ran the better race. When a horse which improved last time and finished fourth where he had not been better than seventh in previous races, an erroneous handicapper may feel that the horse is improving and will be even closer this time. Upon examining *you* may find that there were only five horses in his last race, which means he actually ran no better than his previous outings.

When looking at a closer, it may be very important to know how many horses raced in his last race. The bulkier the field, the more difficult it is for a closer. He is forced to wade through heavy traffic without being blocked in the midst of his drive. The closer who made up ground in a twelve-horse field to finish third, would have to be highly regarded in a seven-horse field where he has running room.

A front runner, on the other hand, may find plenty of company going for the lead in a bulky field. You would have to assume that the more horses there are, the more will want the lead. This makes it more difficult for a *true* front runner to establish a clear early lead without pressure. He may find it easier in his next start with seven horses, when only one other challenges him in the first two furlongs.

Some racetracks have a shortage of horses and the majority of their races are with short fields. When these horses move to a track such as Gulfstream in the winter where they face full fields each time, their successes may be few. You must at least recognize when a horse has been against large or short fields, and use this in your handicapping. It is another tool to be used, and at times can be just the one you need.

Trackman's comments

In the *Daily Racing Form,* just before the number of horses in the last race, there is listed the handicapper's comment of what happened to the horse in his last race.

The comment is narrowed to a word or two, and can indicate when a horse may have had an excuse for losing. You can use these comments to further confirm that a horse had bad racing luck in his last, or whether he had no excuse. These comments are very helpful and should never be overlooked. Use them to confirm a conviction of his last race or, more, to add an insight which you could not have known. There is no better way to tell what happened to a horse on its last time out than to observe it yourself; but if you missed this, the comment can be helpful.

Along these lines, a good handicapper watches a race very closely. Not only does he see *his* horse, but what happens to other horses in the race. You should be able to watch a race and see just about everything that happens without focusing solely on your bet.

When horses that were in trouble run next time, your mental or written note of that occurrence may put you onto a solid longshot winner. Learn to recognize when a horse actually could have done better with better racing luck.

Do not be prejudiced into believing that your horse would have won with better luck when actually he would not have. Many people stick with horses time and again, giving them imaginary excuses for losing when, in actuality, they ran poorly.

CHAPTER 20

Racing record

Just above the actual past performance lines of a horse listed in *Daily Racing Form* will be found the racing record covering the past two years. This record indicates the number of starts made in each of his past two racing years, followed by the number of wins, seconds, and thirds. To the far right of this column will be found the amount of money earned by the horse for each year.

It also lists the lifetime racing record, record over the track being raced at, lifetime turf and wet track records, and the record at today's distance.

This variable shows one important factor, and may aid in pointing out another. First, it shows what sort of consistency the horse has. How often does he win in relation to his starts, and how often does he finish in the money? These are vital because they indicate the animal's habits and show the tenacity he may have. When a horse shows a definite liking for winning, or at least being close most of the time, he is said to be consistent. It makes him more predictable and tells you that when he runs, he *tries*.

Many trainers and jockeys believe that racehorses have personalities and are aware of what is going on. Some desire to extend themselves and win. Some are very competitive and try to beat other horses in a race. Some have more heart and run better despite minor aches and pains than do others.

Many trainers speak of the *intelligence* of a horse. Better horses are often referred to as being intelligent, and these are more easily trained and understand what the game is all about.

Thus the handicapper should seek horses that have shown a tendency to *try*. It would seem a poor risk to back a horse that has had one win in thirty starts and few seconds and thirds. Unless the horse has been running over his head, he has little desire to win. Only rarely do the conditions become right for him to get home first. Such are more easily discouraged and will not extend themselves as will the guttier horse.

When I find a horse that has not shown ability to finish in the money with regularity, before I put my money on him I must feel that he is either taking a drastic class drop, or that the rest of the horses have the same tendencies.

As in baseball, I wouldn't want to wager that a certain batter would get a hit if his batting average showed that he hit only once in thirty tries. I back horses that have shown—when conditions are right—that they will make a run for it. By following past performances, you may find a pattern that indicates when they are properly placed, they perform well.

When a horse shows great consistency, such as fifteen times in the money in seventeen tries with eight wins, I have confidence in him. This horse takes a lot of the guesswork from handicapping. You feel certain the if he is properly placed he will run his best. He tries hard—a guarantee you fail to get with many horses.

Trainers agree that horses develop losing habits, too. A horse placed over his head again and again, that runs far back, has no confidence and may not even win when he *can* outrun the other horses. He may begin to feel inferior and sulk and rarely run hard. This belief is shared by every trainer. Although horses do not speak, I feel the trainers can get an awareness as to the attitude of the horses.

The less a horse is consistent, the greater the risk in wagering on him. Because horse racing is a game of percentages, it doesn't make sense to back horses that win at a poor percentage. When you are betting a quinella or an exacta, you may be just as concerned as to how often he finishes at least second as you would be on his winning. If one horse, for example, has had twenty starts with one win and seven seconds, I would have confidence in him in a quinella or an exacta on the bottom. If I were a show bettor, and a horse has had one win, one second and ten thirds in twenty starts, I would consider him strongly for show. Wherever you hope the horse finishes determines what percentage you are looking for. It certainly makes sense to feel that a horse that has one win and one second in thirty-five starts is a bad quinella or exacta risk.

There are naturally times when you play inconsistent horses. But in general these should be recognized for what they are and considered poor risks. A heavy player who spots his plays may never want to take his chances with the inconsistent horse. One who plays every race may back one now and then, but not with the mortgage money.

The "money earned" column is a tool used by many handicappers to determine class. Their theory is that the horse which has earned the most money per start, or win, or whatever, has a class advantage. This *may* be true, but money earned is more an indicator of the purse structure of the track raced, than the class of company kept.

Let me elaborate. The more money earned, the higher the purses raced for. It is not necessarily an indication of the better grade of horses.

Some tracks offer more purses than others when both races about the same caliber of horses. Emerald Downs in Washington, for example, has an excellent purse structure, better than other minor Western tracks such as Turf Paradise and Arapahoe.

Yet Emerald horses that ship to Turf Paradise for the winter races win with limited success at the same claiming price. Most Emerald horses have earned more money per start than any horses competing in New Mexico or Colorado during the summer. But in the long run, they fare no better.

Emerald horses, on the other hand, do very well when racing at Golden Gate Fields or Bay Meadows where the purses are even higher. An Emerald horse will show a lower average in money earned when moving south for the winter than the horses that have been campaigning in northern California. This in no way indicates the brand of racing they have competed against.

Many other factors determine the purses at racetracks. Most states are trying to upgrade their breeding program; these pay higher purses to state-bred races. In New Jersey, a $5,000 state-bred race will carry a higher purse than a $5,000 claiming race for open competition. A horse that has competed on a regular basis with New Jersey-breds will show a better money-earned average than the non-New Jersey-bred, although the state-bred races are easier because of restriction entries.

All this proves is that the average money earned does not *necessarily* mean that a horse has more class. It can be very misleading at times. There are occasions in which it *is* an indication of class. Take, for example, a horse that has run ten times in 1997 without success, and no 1996 races appear in the past performances.

A look at his 1996 record indicates that he won one race and finished second once. He earned $7,500. If this were a $5,000 claiming race, you would have to believe that at one time the horse had some class. He may not be anywhere near the horse he was, but if he seemed to be regaining some form, you might believe that he can return to some of his previous performances.

The class of horses is a "now" thing. You cannot be concerned with what a horse was able to do two or three years ago, or sometimes even a few months ago. If a horse has raced a number of times without success for $7,500, you have to believe that he may not be more than a $5,000 horse even if he won against allowance competition many races back. He may eventually regain his old form if he is still a young horse, but, in general, you must determine his class from what he has done *lately*.

The best time to use the money-earned average is when handicapping unfamiliar horses that have campaigned against one another over a period of time.

If you were at a strange track and did not know one horse from another, and most of the horses have been competing at the track, you might determine which horses had been running for the better purses by their average winnings. Or when horses are shipping in to a track you are familiar with, and you know that the track was similar in racing caliber, then you might use the earnings to give you an idea of what type of company the horse has kept.

All in all, the money-earned average tells you more about the purse structure of a previous track than the actual class of the horse. Those handicappers who take this average and use it exclusively to determine class are making a big error. It may determine class, or it may *not* determine it. I wouldn't want to bet this way.

When horses have present form and show that they can handle $6,500 company at a particular track, that is good enough for me regardless of what they earned before arriving. The money-earned average should be used *only* when one is unfamiliar with the horse and his past and it may give you a lead as to his true ability.

The use of the racing record should always be used in making your selections. You must ascertain whether the horse is likely to give you his best when the conditions imply he might win. Under perfect conditions, the inconsistent horse may still disappoint you, the consistent horse will disappoint you far less and will give you a far greater return. And if you are a heavy player, forget the inconsistent ones except on rare occasions. A large class drop may be the only time to expect inconsistent horses to win, and even then, not often.

CHAPTER 21

Latest workouts

L isted just below the past performance lines in *Daily Racing Form* is a series of latest workouts. There may be as few as one workout listed, or as many as eight. This depends on how often the horse has worked and at what track you are handicapping. Latest workouts are direct indications of the present physical fitness of a horse and are extremely important to handicapping.

An athlete becomes physically fit by two means, training and competition. Having a Masters degree in Physical Education and having been a three-sport coach for many years gives me an excellent working knowledge of the progression of physical fitness.

A physically unfit horse has little chance of winning. At times, when a horse has far too much class for the field he is asked to beat, he may win when out of peak form. Even the best could not win without any training at all. Could a baseball pitcher go nine innings his first time on the mound after a winter layoff? He would need training and then competition before he would be expected to be at his best for the distance. Even after training, he is rarely ready to pitch nine innings until he has pitched in competition a few times in short spans.

A racehorse has similar problems. He is an athlete and must be trained. Although it is easier for a horse to win the first time back after being in training than it is for a pitcher, the majority of horses need to *compete* before they are ready to win.

A handicapper needs to realize that most of the horses coming back after a layoff lose; many of them are not even asked to run hard. The trainer knows the horse may not be ready and does not wish to hurt him. He may instruct the jockey to win if he can, but do not punish the horse. It is unlikely the horse will win without the urging of the rider. Also, if two things bring an athlete into peak condition, training and competition, it shouldn't be expected of a horse to be ready to win without the second half of the tandem.

When deciding whether a horse is fit enough to win, the handicapper must look at two things. First his latest races; second his workouts. When a horse has been running, his workouts may be of little importance. But at times these can point out a horse ready to win.

When a horse has been away from the races for at least two months, you want to see how he has been training. You would be interested in the frequency of his workouts, and the speed at which he has been working. Of the two, the frequency would be the most important.

I will analyze a horse's return to racing. First, I expect to see a number of workouts—at least three. If a horse has not raced in six months or so, two workouts would leave me suspicious. Could I get my team ready with two practices? If he had been away only two or three months, I may feel a bit safer. He may not have been laid up, just resting, and would not need as much training to regain form.

Looking at the longer layoff, three workouts may be sufficient, more would be better. During those workouts I would hope to see at least one beyond four furlongs. I would be looking for the trainer to build some stamina into a horse. I would also hope to see at least one short workout to build up some speed, especially if the horse is expected to sprint.

The times of the workouts may not be of great importance. I would like them to be relatively fast, but they need not be speedy. When working three furlongs, at most tracks, anything under :36 seconds is fast. Under :35 is moving very well. The lower the time from that point on, the faster the work. Between :36 and :38 is fair. Over :38 should indicate the horse was not pushed. If he was, he's in trouble. At four furlongs, under :48 is fast. Under :47 is better and so on. From :48 to :50 is fair, with :50 being on the slow side.

Going five furlongs when working under 1:01 is good. Under 1:00 is fast and over 1:01 is slower, but consider that it was a long workout meant to build stamina and is useful.

In six-furlong works or over, one may compare the normal running time at the track for six furlongs and judge how good the work was. You naturally wouldn't expect a horse to work out as fast as a race is run, so anything just over that would be good.

The important thing with long workouts is the trainer's intention of building stamina and the time becomes less important. When you see a fast, long workout, you know the horse is ready, but a slow, long workout must be considered helpful.

Workouts are listed along with other information about the work. The clocker will estimate how easily the horse was running while establishing his time. The clocker may list it as breezing, meaning they barely let the horse run; handily, meaning they let him out a bit, but still under restraint; or driving which would indicate he was working hard. Rarely have I ever seen a clocker list a workout other than breezing or handily. Some clockers have a tendency to put the same thing for nearly all workouts, which would mean that the small "b" or "h" listed by the workout is meaningless.

Other information about workouts may show that he worked out from the starting gate. Many people feel that the workout from a gate should be slower because his break is inhibited by the gate, just as in an actual race. This may not be true, however, as the clocker usually begins timing at the flag just after the break. This would mean that the horse has a running start as in a workout without the gate and his time would be the same. The "g" shown next to the workout indicates working from the gate, and may be important when a horse has had some bad habits breaking in recent races.

For example, a horse that has reared or hesitated for a race or two may show a few workouts subsequently from the starting gate. This, at least, would indicate that the trainer is trying to correct his problem, or that the starter has ordered additional training from the gate. Under either circumstance, if the work is fast it may indicate that his gate problems have been licked.

Horses may also work in company with other horses, which would be closer to race conditions. The letter "c" would appear by the workout indicating this. A workout in company may be a bit faster because of the competition, but should be considered a favorable event. Workouts are also conducted in training races. Training races may have between four and six starters and should be considered good conditioners for the horse.

When the track is muddy, or when the inside of the surface is meant to be protected for one reason or another by the track superintendent, markers or cones will be placed, removed from the inner rail far enough so as to protect what they hoped to protect. This is listed in the *Form* as "dogs up."

Horses working with dogs up must run outside the cones thereby running a bit farther in their work. A workout on a track with dogs up is likely to be slower for two reasons. One is that the track is likely to be off; the other is that they must run wide around the cones.

Besides the problems of interpreting workouts, one must realize that all workouts are not recorded by the clockers. At many tracks the clockers must recognize the horses by markings, exercise riders, colors or any other way of determining who is working. The trainer need not report to the clocker so the clocker is on his own in defining who and how fast the work was. At other tracks, each horse must be announced to the clocker telling how far he will work. This eliminates missed workouts and is a far more reliable system.

At a large track such as Monmouth Park, as many as 250 horses have worked on a given morning. Because of the sheer volume, the accuracy of the published workouts is somewhat questionable; but for the most part it can be trusted.

Most tracks have a rule that no horse is allowed to race unless it has at least one published workout within a certain time period, usually 45 days. Any horse without these published works is not allowed to run.

One other concern of workouts is that sometimes the trainers do not work their horses at the track at which they are racing. They may have a training track at their disposal and only bring the horse to the track for his final two workouts. These may be short and slow, leading one to believe he is not in shape. Such ploys are used by trainers to keep the shrewd bettors away from their horses.

All in all, you must make use of what you know and don't try to guess. If a horse shows workouts sufficient to believe he is in condition, you have something to go on. The time may not be that important to older horses, just the fact that they have worked. If they show no works, or one or two slow and short works, you have no way of telling whether they are in shape or not and can't make an accurate judgement. This horse should not be played, and if you are afraid he will win, but can't play him, skip the race.

The times recorded in workouts are more significant when handicapping first-time starters. The trainers, for the most part, do not know how fast the horse can run unless they test him. If he shows no fast workouts it means one of two things. One is that he is not fast. Two is that he was worked elsewhere and they are just keeping him fit and eligible with his published works.

If a first-time starter has fast works, it should tell you he can run. If his works are slow, it *may* man he can't run. As you can see, wagering on first-time starters is precarious. There is too much you don't know and can't find out. Only personal relationships with the trainers can fill in the unknown, but most handicappers do not have access to the trainers and can only use *Daily Racing Form*—which will not have that information.

When a horse has been running on a regular basis, workouts have a slightly different meaning. If a horse runs every two weeks or so, he may not show any works between races. Either he doesn't need them, is galloped at a slow pace to maintain fitness, or is unable to work because of soreness. A horse that runs regularly may show a work or two between races. *The time of these works is of no importance, especially if they are slow.* The trainer knows how fast the horse can run and only works him to keep him fit. *A fast work **may** be significant.* If the horse seems to be improving and suddenly he works four furlongs in :46-2, you may feel he is sharp and ready for a top effort.

Horses that run far back all the time may show fast works and still run badly in a race. I tend to go more by their past races than by a sudden fast workout. If his races were hopeless, even a fast work won't convince me. A horse that has been racing and is eligible to improve, who suddenly works fast, may be a good play.

Workouts between races are always good to see because they tell the horse is probably sound and can stand training. *No* works between races could possibly indicate some unsoundness and make playing him more risky.

As I mentioned earlier, the most difficult thing to assess is the fitness of a horse that has laid up from three to six weeks with no works. At three weeks I may feel he is still in form; every day after that I become more and more suspicious.

When I can't definitely say that a horse is physically fit to win, I don't have a solid play. There is no way of knowing—other than seeing the techniques of the trainer—when a horse that has not raced in a month and shows one or no workouts is physically fit. When you are confronted with this common problem, recognize it and treat it properly. Heavy bettors—

beware; small ones—tread lightly. When you have unanswered questions, you have a weak wager.

No horse *at any time* is a solid play when a question of fitness cannot be answered. When it is determined that he is not fit, he can easily be eliminated from further consideration. Fitness should be your first determination. You can go no further with a horse until you make that decision.

Morning workouts directly relate to the physical fitness of a horse. Study the workouts, and from them, along with his racing past, decide his present fitness.

Remember that all the other variables such as class, time, speed rating, post position, etc. are all meaningless if the horse is not physically fit. Make sure you keep the horse before the cart and answer that question first; *then* go.

CHAPTER 22

Putting it all together

I have spent the past 21 chapters writing about the variables that go into making a selection in a horse race. *Every variable discussed and interpreted in this book is one listed by Daily Racing Form.*

There may be other variables that could be a factor in handicapping. I am certain that one could come up with at least twenty more possibilities. *The significance of such variables would be the major question.* Does it pay to be bogged down with many factors when handicapping, most of which have only a remote chance of affecting the outcome? I think not.

I strongly recommend keeping it simple. You have enough trouble understanding the important things without spending time on the remote.

I have been asked many strange questions over the years about the effect of certain conditions. Something like the wind factor may have some effect on a race, but the racing fan is generally not equipped to determine the exact effect the wind will have on each horse. Unless a definite pattern exists, I would ignore the wind factor and look for the best horses.

There are enough problems in interpreting and evaluating the factors at your disposal. Do not be worried about the less significant facts that are not at your disposal. Within the confines of *Daily Racing Form*, there is enough information to select sufficient winners to win money at the races. Why complicate matters by bringing in confusing aspects that only tend to cloud up an already unclear picture?

One can never be absolutely *sure* as to the outcome of any horse race. One must be satisfied to produce a percentage of winners sufficient to make a profit. Although no one race is sure, a series of races should bring the good handicapper a predictable amount of success if he follows good, sound principles, as outlined in this book.

Handicapping is not simple, but simpler than many people make it. I do not envy the handicapper who spends his time comparing live and deadweight, the wind factor and whether a horse worked out around the dogs or not. These factors may have a significance, but are very difficult to incorporate into your handicapping, and can never outweigh the important things.

One should spend the moments of handicapping in trying to answer the two basic questions of *fitness* and *class*. When the non-contenders are dismissed, one can put the remaining variables to use in separating the field until he comes up with a solid play.

In putting your knowledge to use, I recommend the process of elimination. Begin by eliminating those horses you believe to be unfit, or lacking in class.

From what is left, begin incorporating the rest of the variables. Continue to eliminate by disposing of those horses racing at the wrong distance; or which have an unplayable jockey; or a heavy weight burden or a bad post position; or a running style not conducive to a top performance in the race.

Then compare, if need be, by using variables such as fractional times, previous odds, number of horses in previous races, etc.

A recent workout may catch the eye, or a good trainer may sway you.

All in all, use every tool you can logically use to narrow down a field when the answer is less obvious.

Ideally, I will narrow down the field by the use of common sense and basic handicapping principles, to one horse—and hopefully he will win.

In further elaborating on the important process of elimination, let us assume you narrow a field to three contenders. If you expect to play just one, you must ignore the ones previously eliminated and concentrate on comparing the three remaining. As you continue to compare, you may eliminate one more.

When you are down to two horses in a non-quinella or exacta race, you end up with alternatives. You may play both, providing the odds are sufficient to make a profit, or you can choose between the two.

If you're from the school that believes betting two horses in a race is taboo, you will likely make the wrong decision half the time. This will cut down on winning, but will also cut down on the losses when playing both horses. So it may end up the same in the long run. Naturally, when you can get down to one horse, you have no problem.

In quinella and exacta handicapping, you need not narrow down the field as finely. Getting a field down to three may be as far as you need to go. Six dollars in a quinella and twelve dollars in an exacta can tie up all three horses.

I would like to caution you to be not overly influenced by the tote board. Many times a horse is rationally eliminated from contention by the handicapper; but, upon seeing the juicy large odds at race time, he begins to re-evaluate the animal. He starts seeing things that are not there and decides to play the animal.

My suggestion is to forget the horses you've thrown out and concentrate on the remainder. It is easier to compare three horses than ten. The few times you win on a horse after changing your mind because of odds will be more than lost back in the long run.

I can see only two exceptions in allowing the odds to sway you. One is when your selection's odds are so low that it is not worthwhile to wager on him. *In this case, skip the race.* Secondly, if a horse you feel is a contender goes off at unusually long odds, you may play him despite the fact he was not your first choice. The horse, however, must have been considered a contender and not one you decided had no chance in your original calculations.

Changing your mind is very dangerous for a horse player. It always seems that when you change your mind you end up on the short end. There are times, however, you *must* change your mind—but only due to unforeseen factors.

The appearance of a horse prior to the race is very important. I rarely wager on a horse dripping with perspiration and apparently nervous. One should never wager on a horse without seeing him. I will only ignore the perspiring horse when it is very hot and most of the other horses are sweating; or when I've seen a horse perspire before and win.

Sweaty and nervous horses are poor plays and most trainers will readily reveal they hate to see their horses washy. They usually feel that something is bothering the horse to make him nervous. This is usually enough to make him finish up the track. Especially, stay away from horses that are usually dry before the race, then suddenly appear washy. Here again is the advantage of being a regular at a track; you have the opportunity to recognize this.

Bandages are also a controversial issue among horse players. Many feel that the bandages are used to support broken-down legs and that the horse is a bad risk. In interviewing trainers, most reveal that the bandages are primarily for *protection*. Many horses kick themselves and need to be bandaged to prevent cuts and abrasions.

In some cases, however, they are for support and can mean the horse is not sound.

They are for support and can mean the horse is not sound.

I especially avoid horses that have been away for a long time, drop in class, and appear on the track in heavy front bandages. Rear bandages have little significance since horses land on their front legs harder.

If, in general, I am suspicious about the soundness of an animal, I do not like to see front bandages. If the horse has raced with bandages before, or is a classy animal, or if there is no reason to believe he is unsound, I ignore the bandages.

Bandages look worse than they are, and I have at times gotten off of winners because of their bandaged appearance. I think we should give some credit to the veterinarians on the job and assume that broken-down horses are not competing.

One thing a handicapper *must* learn to do is to make decisions. Many tickets are cashed or ripped up because of a right or wrong decision. This is part of the game. I suggest making a decision and sticking to it. A horse player can have no better friend than his own convictions. If they turn out to be wrong, examine your decision to see if you would do the same thing if they were still selling tickets. When you make a mistake, recognize it, and learn from it. It is important to be open-minded enough to realize your mistakes.

Remember, there are a hundred ways for a horse to *lose* a race, and your handicapping may have been correct even when losing. Conversely, if you were wrong, don't try to make phony excuses for losing. When you do this you usually get back on the same horses over and over again despite the fact they lost over and over again.

Handicapping is a very humbling experience. Have confidence in your selections and your ability, but do *not* be cocky. Victory plants the seed of defeat. Overconfidence brews complacency and laziness. Don't let overconfidence take the place of hard work and thoroughness.

Remember, no one is the world's greatest handicapper—although many profess to be. There are many great handicappers found at every track in the country, all equally good in their own way, and all capable of winning money. The man who runs about after a winning race yelling "I'm the world's greatest handicapper," will soon find out he is not.

Handicapping is a continuous learning process. You should never be satisfied that you know enough. Hope to be better next year than you were this year. Do not become discouraged when losing.

Just as in athletics, you have ups and downs. Learn to ride the waves. Prolonged losing streaks may mean you are doing something wrong and you need to make changes and corrections in your techniques. Short losing streaks are common and happen to everyone. Take them in stride. Continue to read, study, and learn to be humble; tomorrow you may learn something.

I have found handicapping to be the single most gratifying thing I've ever done. Every day brings a new challenge, every race an experience. I can see myself being as excited about it twenty years from now as I am now. I only wish everyone the same enjoyment and success I've had.

See you trackside, and good handicapping to you!

About the Author

Chuck Badone is an expert handicapper. He first pursued it as a hobby. After many years of research, Badone turned his race handicapping talents into a profession. The former teacher-coach holds two Masters degrees in education. He is now the resident handicapper at Lone Star Park at Grand Prairie.

Badone conducts handicapping seminars, presents thoughtful selections between races and picks winners for the *Fort Worth Star-Telegram*.

This revised edition of his classic book on handicapping covers every aspect of the handicapping thoroughbred races. This book can be used as a guide by both veteran and novice racegoers and will be a valuable addition to any racing library.

It will help bring out the big winner inside you!

CPSIA information can be obtained
at www.ICGtesting.com
Printed in the USA
BVOW09s1659230218
508711BV00001B/43/P